WITHDRAWN

Why Am I Afraid To Tell You I'm a Christian?

Witnessing Jesus' Way

Don Posterski

InterVarsity Press
Downers Grove
Illinois 60515

© 1983 by Inter-Varsity Christian Fellowship of the United States of America

All rights reserved. No part of this book may be reproduced in any form without written permission from InterVarsity Press, Downers Grove, Illinois.

InterVarsity Press is the book-publishing division of Inter-Varsity Christian Fellowship, a student movement active on campus at hundreds of universities, colleges and schools of nursing. For information about local and regional activities, write IVCF, 233 Langdon St., Madison, WI 53703.

Distributed in Canada through InterVarsity Press, 860 Denison St., Unit 3, Markham, Ontario L3R 4H1, Canada.

Cover cartoon: Rob Suggs

All Scripture quotations marked NIV are taken from the Holy Bible: New International Version. Copyright © 1978 by the New York International Bible Society. Used by permission of Zondervan Bible Publishers.

All Scripture quotations marked RSV are from the Revised Standard Version of the Bible, copyrighted 1946, 1952, © 1971, 1973.

ISBN 0-87784-847-5

Printed in the United States of America

Library of Congress Cataloging in Publication Data
Posterski, Don.
    Why am I afraid to tell you I'm a Christian?

    1. Evangelistic work. 2. Witness bearing
(Christianity) I. Title.
BV3790.P653   1983   248'.5   83-12958
ISBN 0-87784-847-5

16	15	14	13	12	11	10	9	8	7	6	5	4	3	2	1
95	94	93	92	91	90	89	88	87	86	85	84	83			

To Beth—
friend and companion...
to the end

Foreword

Evangelism for most people is a dreaded subject. We have many caricatures of evangelists. Most of them are negative. Deep down our basic fear is that we cannot at the same time be sensitive to people's needs and evangelize. Witnessing appears to be an intrusion into other people's lives. For some, evangelism is not consistent with the modern world in which we live.

This book talks about how evangelism fits into life. Don Posterski offers to you his hard-learned convictions about sharing the gospel with people. He shows you how evangelism fits into the total Christian life. Here is witness Jesus style.

Don writes in a personal way. He acts the way he writes. He communicates the Christian faith personally.

Don is one of the leaders of Inter-Varsity Christian Fellowship in Canada. Inter-Varsity is committed to evangelism in the context of real life. The content of the gospel is to express truth and to demonstrate love.

The objectives of Inter-Varsity in Canada can be summarized in five words:

☐ evangelism
☐ discipleship
☐ love
☐ truth
☐ mission

Don has woven all five of these objectives together. This book is significant in that it brings forth fresh thinking on word and deed, truth and love, in evangelistic communication.

I urge you to read this book carefully. Christians in North America need to have Don's heart for the gospel, its content and action.

James E. Berney
General Director
Inter-Varsity Christian Fellowship of Canada

Preface

Evangelism has been an emotional issue for me. The subject has sent me on enough guilt trips to travel around the world. This book is a result of my

☐ wrestling with God,

☐ disagreeing with high-conformity evangelistic methods, and

☐ trying to figure out how to be both biblical and faithful.

You will notice that footnotes and references are absent. My research has been by the osmosis method in the laboratory of life. I am indebted to many sources. The material in this book has resulted from readings, studies of the life of Jesus, discussions, ideas seeded at conferences, experiments with university students, personal experiences, and teachings from people who have influenced me.

My focus is on Jesus. I want to study our Lord's approach and articulate his manner and method as a model for sharing the faith. I see his human example as the ideal for those who follow him and share his mission.

Training in evangelism often restricts the scope of the gospel to subjects directly tied to Jesus and the cross. Using Jesus as a model expands the content of our witness to all matters of truth and life. This book offers a method. My aim is to encourage followers of Jesus to

☐ listen before they speak,

☐ discern what others believe,

☐ communicate with people rather than deliver impersonal messages, and

☐ think about the process as well as the decision.

Jesus repeatedly adapted his message to fit the situation and the person. He translated his teaching theory into tangible acts of love that touched people's needs. Doing things his way can be our way to be faithful representatives and to find personal freedom too.

1

JESUS THE EVANGELIST: HIS MANNER AND METHOD

I used to feel like someone at a formal banquet dressed in a swimsuit when I tried to witness. I felt embarrassed. My words didn't always fit the situation. They were sometimes forced on people rather than being a response to people. I lacked the art of putting the gospel in contact with real life. When I tried to connect Jesus with our modern world, I was unnatural. I was afraid.

Locker-Room Talk
An incident at an Inter-Varsity staff conference lives in my mind as a model of effective witness without trauma. We were sharing a retreat center with a group of high-school

graduates who were on a government work program. Our daily events were completely separate. Other than passing in the halls, the only times we met were in the washrooms. The IV staff used a break in the evening schedule to play a bruising game of broomball. As we hauled our battered bodies to the showers and settled down for a rejuvenating sauna, we met two young men from the other group who were also enjoying the heat and steam. We began talking. My fellow staffer Bill took the lead to find out more about Brian and George. Eventually, the flow of the conversation changed directions, and Brian turned to another staffer, Serge, who spoke only French, and asked, "What do you do?"

Serge made a valiant attempt to use all of the four hundred English words in his vocabulary to communicate a job description of an Inter-Varsity campus staff member. He finally resolved his frustration by stating, "I help students in universities figure out what they believe about God."

Brian and George were surprised, but interested. They asked pursuing questions that Bill and I attempted to answer clearly. Sensing that a bridge had been built between us strong enough to hold our weight, Bill looked at the more vocal Brian and asked, "Have you guys figured out what you believe about God yet?" Significant territory was covered during the next half-hour. The discussion ranged from questioning God's existence to the charge that the Bible is just a human book, from the problem of evil and suffering to the virtues and loopholes in the theory of evolution.

Brian was intrigued by the idea that everyone believes something and that how we behave tips our hand about what we believe. There was laughter, charges and counter-charges, a refreshing level of locker-room talk. Brian and

George were a long way from being convinced that Jesus had any bearing on their personal plans, but I offered to send each of them a book if they would read it. They accepted the idea with modest enthusiasm.

We were having a staff party the following evening so we invited them to come and bring their friends. They accepted and showed up with twenty others. We shared our normal ration of late-night snacks. Cigarette smoke mixed with light and heavy discussions in the room. Only God knows all that happened that night.

In contrast to this time with Brian and George, I remember a Christmas seminar with international students. The seminar subject was "Modern Myths—Illusions People Hinge Their Hopes on in Search of the Good Life." Part of the seminar included small-group sharing about what each person believed. After the official session ended, several groups extended their discussions. When I returned to the meeting room half an hour later, five people were still involved in intense conversation. I slipped into the vacant chair in the circle and watched.

Fifteen minutes of careful listening exposed the group. Of the mix of five graduate students, two were followers of Jesus and three believed otherwise. One German student had deeper insight than his limited English would allow him to explain. The content of the conversation was rich and expressed with deep feelings. Those who were not Christian believers readily offered their reasons for rejecting God as a viable option. They preferred to trust science and technology and their human capacities to cope with the demands of life.

Joe was the verbal Christian in the group. When he spoke, he spoke the truth. But his manner, due to his nervousness, was to deliver speeches. Instead of talking about science or humanism as inadequate belief systems, Joe came on with sermonettes that ended with references to Jesus and the cross. The more often he spoke, the longer he spoke and the more restless his listeners became. Hans, who was from Sweden, had spoken only once, but finally his restlessness took one short step to frustration. "You Christians," he charged, "present your beliefs and religion as a package . . . a proven, quality product that, when used, is guaranteed to make you a better person. Analyzing and questioning is not emphasized. You make me feel like a lousy consumer!"

Hans was right. Joe meant well but discredited the message. He was properly motivated, his intentions were on track, but he was insensitive and what he said was largely irrelevant. Joe was dispensing information rather than listening and then replying to his audience. Jesus would not follow that pattern.

Jesus Our Model

Part of God's purpose in wrapping Jesus in human flesh and allowing him to walk with us in history was to give us a model of how to live. Jesus accepted this role as his responsibility for his years on earth. He affirmed this self-understanding in the upper room when he clearly announced to his disciples, "I have given you an example, that you also should do as I have done" (Jn 13:15 RSV).

Following his resurrection, Jesus extended the responsibility for modeling to his disciples. The commissioning service, again in the upper room, culminated when Jesus asserted, "As the Father has sent me, even so I send you" (Jn 20:21 RSV). Our surrender to Jesus as our model and master teacher includes accepting his manner of witness. We seek to reproduce his pattern. What Jesus incarnated, we strive with the help of his Spirit to re-incarnate. In terms of our own style of witness, then, our aim is to be like Jesus.

Jesus did practice personal evangelism and he did have a technique. His approach was to deal with no two people in the same way. He personalized the message so it connected with the individuals involved. If his manner can be interpreted as a method, he stated truth that was tailored to the specific situation. He wrapped his subject matter around the person and the occasion like a cover on a baseball.

Xerox evangelism was not Jesus' way. His approach escaped artificiality. He refused to record his message on a mental cassette tape and to spend the rest of his life punching buttons that moved his mouth. Instead, Jesus adapted his witness to his audience and the context. He conveyed what was suitable to the occasion.

The biblical record shows that Jesus had something different to say to each person. Perhaps surprisingly, it is only to Nicodemus that Jesus said, "You must be born again" (Jn 3:7 NIV). We have no basis to contend that Jesus offered that particular directive to anyone else. Likewise, his dealings with Zacchaeus (Lk 19:1-10) were radically different from his decree to the rich young ruler (Mk 10:17-22), even though money was the core issue in both instances. His approach to the Samaritan woman and her many husbands (Jn 4:1-30) was distinct from his handling of the woman caught committing adultery (Jn 8:1-11). Jesus' approach was so sensitive and personal that even people who shared blindness were treated differently (Mt 9:27-28 and Mk 8:22-23). He responded with compassion and fed the five thousand who were hungry (Jn 6:1-14), although he reacted with anger and indicted the power-hungry Pharisees (Mt 23:27-28). We are not left guessing about Jesus' style of evangelism. Without compromising the truth, he personalized the message.

Demonstrating Jesus' Style

A case study of Jesus' encounter with the rich ruler and the discussion with his disciples that followed it reinforces the principles Jesus practiced. The biblical account is recorded in Mark 10:17-31 and paralleled in Matthew 19:16-30 and Luke 18:18-30. The whole event is a model for our evangelism. The patterns are guides for us to follow. As we allow Jesus' standards to shape us, our witness will be faithful and effective.

As Jesus started on his way, a man ran up to him and fell on his knees before him. "Good teacher," he asked, "what must I do to inherit eternal life?"

"Why do you call me good?" Jesus answered. "No one is good—except God alone. You know the commandments: 'Do not murder, do not commit adultery, do not steal, do not give false testimony, do not defraud, honor your father and mother.' "

"Teacher," he declared, "all these I have kept since I was a boy."

Jesus looked at him and loved him. "One thing you lack," he said. "Go, sell everything you have and give to the poor, and you will have treasure in heaven. Then come, follow me."

At this the man's face fell. He went away sad, because he had great wealth.

Jesus looked around and said to his disciples, "How hard it is for the rich to enter the kingdom of God!"

The disciples were amazed at his words. But Jesus said again, "Children, how hard it is to enter the kingdom of God! It is easier for a camel to go through the eye of a needle than for a rich man to enter the king-

dom of God."

The disciples were even more amazed, and said to each other, "Who then can be saved?"

Jesus looked at them and said, "With man this is impossible, but not with God; all things are possible with God."

Peter said to him, "We have left everything to follow you!"

"I tell you the truth," Jesus replied, "no one who has left home or brothers or sisters or mother or father or children or fields for me and the gospel will fail to receive a hundred times as much in this present age (homes, brothers, sisters, mothers, children and fields —and with them, persecutions) and in the age to come, eternal life. But many who are first will be last, and the last first." (Mk 10:17-31 NIV)

1. Jesus focused on his audience. The rich ruler had been a listener in the crowd when Jesus claimed that in order to get into the kingdom one had to be like a child. Even though he was young, he was no child and Jesus' teaching troubled him. His money had gained him the extras in this life, and he did not want to miss anything in the next life either.

The young man arrived with a disrupted spirit. He was anxious but still feeling strong. His self-confidence prompted him to aim his first question at the bottom line. "Good teacher, what must I do to inherit eternal life?"

Now Jesus was already leaving the crowd. In his mind, the session was over. He was thinking about the next item on his agenda. But he stopped and gave his full attention to his enquirer. "Slow down, my friend," was Jesus' mood. "Let's handle one item at a time. Why do you call me good? God alone is good. Now, about your question. . . . You know the commandments. . . ."

Jesus repeatedly surrendered himself to his audience. When a crowd was prepared to listen, he was a preacher and teacher. When a debater tested his teachings, he sharpened his mind and tongue. When children came to him, he lifted them to his knees and talked and laughed. When individuals sought his attention, he listened carefully and responded with specifics (Mk 10:1-16).

At least two underlying forces account for Jesus' focus. He was free from preoccupation with himself, and he was acutely conscious of his context. If we are tied up with ourselves, our ability to tune in to our context will be dulled. If our motivation is to control the flow of a conversation, we will either manipulate the person or speak too much and listen too little. If our drive is to impress people with our insight, we will be blinded to the insights of others and deafened to their needs.

We are free to respond with sensitivity to different situations and to contribute to others only when we have been released from ourselves. Even though the disciples were crowded around, Jesus gave the rich ruler his full attention. In spite of the pressure, Jesus was able to give the young man a personal appointment.

2. Jesus signaled his personal care. There was a pause in the discussion between Jesus and the rich ruler before Jesus delivered his bottom line. Jesus knew his counsel to sell all would be hard news for the rich ruler. The disciples must have talked about this at one of their "remember when" reunions. "Remember when Jesus looked at the rich ruler and signaled his love to him?"

Followers of Jesus are called to be *lovers first—witnesses second.* Weaving the right words together in a conversation without wrapping them in personal concern is like throwing tracts out the window of a city bus. Our love for people should flow out of both subjective and objective sources—from both our hearts and heads. On the subjective, heart side, what comes out of us is the result of what God puts in us. Since God is love and his Spirit abides in us, love is in us too. As God's love is passed through us, the expression may come out as emotional warmth or as the power to be patient and kind.

On the objective, head side, love is more conceptual. Love is rooted as an idea and linked to God's conviction (shown in creation) that people have great worth and unique value. Even in the realm of things, we appreciate what has value and do not abuse what has worth. We do not carve our initials on oak coffee tables or slash the upholstery in Cutlass Supreme Oldsmobiles. As we relate to people in friendships, random relationships and chance encounters, our commitment to care is elevated. We avoid slurring college classmates or business colleagues with I-don't-care-about-you attitudes. We are careful not to hurt friends or relatives with harsh words.

Jesus' love for the rich ruler was communicated with both his heart and head. His eyes and voice and posture conveyed compassion and honest concern as his words delivered the message that was true and right.

3. Jesus connected subject and situation. Jesus repeatedly used the context to frame his content. He used the normal events of his days to teach his truth. We do not hear him speaking on a master tape and then running duplicates. He was constantly connecting his subject matter with people's questions or needs and their unique circumstances. The conversation with the rich ruler and the discussion which followed illustrates Jesus' pattern.

Remember—the rich ruler arrived before Jesus with a

confident self-image. He was young and energetic, a clean-living and religious type. His power, position and wealth made him a desirable disciple. He might have anticipated affirmation from Jesus, maybe even public commendation. At first the discussion with Jesus progressed close to his expectations. He sensed that Jesus liked him. Then suddenly the conversation moved to the matter of money. The price for Jesus' kind of eternal life was too high. The young ruler didn't want to leave but he knew he couldn't stay.

This event was also unsettling for the disciples. They began wondering about the level of their commitments. Although Jesus might have preferred some time to reflect, he seized the moment to teach. The subject matter was money and the rich.

"How hard it is for the rich to enter the kingdom of God." The statement staggered the Twelve so Jesus repeated himself and added a verbal picture. "Children, how hard it is to enter the kingdom of God! It is easier for a camel to go through the eye of a needle than for a rich man to enter the kingdom of God."

A couple of the disciples may have laughed at Jesus' ludicrous image, but the majority must have wondered, "Who then can be saved?" Jesus knew this was the moment to tell the whole crew that God the Father was the only one who could save anybody.

Peter's mind was still hung up on Jesus' demand to the young ruler to sell everything, and he blurted out, "We did sell everything. We have nothing left to give."

Jesus knew that now the time for reassurance had arrived, and he moved in for the final word. "My friends, you have given up a lot, but let me tell you another truth. In this life, you will receive a hundred times more than you have given up, and eternal life is still to come when the first will be last and the last first."

As each situation developed, Jesus would move the conversation to its natural conclusions. In a single event, Jesus

☐ announced that God alone is good,

☐ declared the terms of salvation for the rich ruler,

☐ taught his disciples the truth about money,

☐ pronounced God's role in salvation,

☐ promised rich blessings to those who are committed, and

☐ assured his distressed followers that justice would prevail in the end.

The scenario with the rich ruler was not an exception for Jesus. A study of the New Testament reveals Jesus consistently adapting his witness to people in particular situations.

☐ Over dinner, when he was criticized by his Pharisee host for not washing before he ate, he used the situation spontaneously. "Now you Pharisees cleanse the outside of the cup and of the dish, but inside you are full of extortion and wickedness" (Lk 11:39 RSV). The discussion that followed was hot. The danger of being preoccupied with externals while minimizing one's internal condition was important to Jesus.

☐ During a walking tour of Jerusalem with his disciples, Jesus' conversation led to comments about the beautiful stones in the walls of the temple. Jesus used the occasion to prophesy and teach about the end times. "The time will come," he said, "when not one stone will be left on another" (Lk 21:6 NIV).

☐ During one of his heavy teaching days with a large crowd, Jesus opened himself up for questions and discussions. (If Jesus were on a university speaking tour in our time, he would probably use the same format.)

Someone in the crowd requested, "Teacher, tell my brother to divide the inheritance with me." Jesus refused to be an arbitrator and again jumped at the opportunity to warn about greed. He concluded with the punch line that "a man's life does not consist in the abundance of his possessions" (Lk 12:13-15 NIV).

☐ One afternoon on the way to Capernaum, the disciples had an internal squabble about who would have position and power when Jesus set up his kingdom. Instead of being pushed to despair by their ignorance or lecturing the Twelve, Jesus used the opportunity to press his point on servanthood. "If anyone wants to be first, he must be the very last, and the servant of all" (Mk 9:35 NIV).

☐ Jesus applied his personal touch to Nicodemus. A teacher and informed member of the Sanhedrin, Nicodemus was treated as a knowledgeable religious leader. Jesus' manner was assertive. His language was fit for a synagogue. Nicodemus was invited to be "born again" (Jn 3:1-15).

☐ On the occasion when Jesus was a guest at the home of Mary and Martha, dissension broke out over priorities. Martha was cooking in the kitchen and emotionally steaming while Mary was talking with Jesus in the living room. When Martha appealed to Jesus for Mary's assistance, he condoned Mary's priority to eat spiritual truth rather than Martha's concern to prepare physical food (Lk 10:38-41).

☐ Jesus took initiative toward Levi, the tax collector, with a direct call to believe and follow him. Levi responded and later arranged for Jesus to be the guest of honor at an evangelistic dinner party for his tax collector colleagues. Surely the evening included a testimonial from Levi and Jesus as the main speaker. How did Jesus begin his address? He started with "tax talk" on the way to his main point (Lk 5:27-32).

Another obvious pattern in Jesus' communication style was parables. He was a master storyteller. His creative mind transmitted visual signals. He knew illustrations painted mental pictures that his listeners would remember and repeat. Jesus' storytelling style is an invitation for us to be imaginative as we retell the truth in our time.

Wherever Jesus went he taught the truth revealed to him by his Father in heaven. His grasp of God's ways allowed him to tailor his truth and personalize his messages. As a result, his content was variable and always seemed to touch his audience. Tracking Jesus' style reminds us that his witness was not restricted to information about the cross and his impending death. His witness extended to the full range of individual interests and concerns. His only restriction was to stay within the boundaries defined by truth itself.

4. Jesus enjoyed discussions. The biblical accounts of events involving Jesus are accurate. They faithfully inform us of what actually happened. We can stake our lives on their truthfulness. The accuracy of the written record, however, must not be confused with the completeness of the account. If all the words Jesus articulated in his teachings were combined with the private explanations his disciples heard, the New Testament would approximate the *Encyclopaedia Britannica.* The Bible is not like the Congressional Record or Hansard's record of parliament or a court reporter's account of a legal case. The Bible is a summary statement—accurate and truthful, but incomplete. It is like a seventy-page compendium of a four-day conference.

Jesus was a highly verbal person. When he wasn't healing and dealing with demons, he was talking. His days were filled with dialog. If he wasn't asking questions, he was answering them. If he wasn't teaching, he was clarifying his teachings. Spontaneous debates were the highlights of Jesus' day. He interacted with children and adults with equal ease. At a party or in the synagogue, Jesus excelled in the art of conversation and enjoyed discussion.

The written record of Jesus' encounter with the rich ruler is a skeleton of the whole. We can legitimately read between the lines. The subjects Jesus addressed with the young ruler and the clarification that followed with his disciples probably took longer than the two minutes required to read the biblical account.

The point is that Jesus was not a hit-and-run evangelist who hurled verbal pronouncements at people and then moved on to his next appointment. Even the reduced scriptural statement involving the rich ruler shows Jesus asking and answering questions, interacting in conversation and even transmitting his feelings before he announced the terms of true commitment.

5. Jesus touched control centers. The rich ruler had received a fair hearing. But as he physically walked away from Jesus, his mind stayed behind. Jesus' charge pounded inside his head. "One thing you lack. . . . Go and sell. . . . And follow me."

The young man stopped and pondered. "Does Jesus know what he is demanding? Does he misunderstand? What does he mean, 'You will have treasure in heaven?' Can't a person have both? What's wrong with being rich? I know—I'll offer Jesus half my fortune. He could use the money." For just a moment, the young ruler may have contemplated returning for a second session with Jesus. He stopped walking and stood in silence but something inside him would not let him turn around.

"Sell ... give ... then come back. ... One thing you lack," Jesus had charged. With a troubled spirit, the young man started walking again. "Jesus was right. I'll stick with my money ... a better bet anyway," he reasoned. And he started to walk faster.

Jesus might have been content to start a discussion by talking about the weather. But conversational doodling did not go far enough. The stakes were too high. Separation from his Father was too consequential. Social etiquette that ruled out tempering with the real issues in life had to be set aside. Jesus knew what he was doing with the rich ruler. He touched the control center of his life. He fingered the young man's true god. Money was the power that ruled him. And both Jesus and the young man knew they had to go separate ways.

6. *Jesus placed truth above results.* Jesus was left with a troubled spirit as well. There was no desire to negotiate a compromise. He simply was disappointed. "Another triumph for Satan," Jesus may have thought with disgust. "The young man had such promise. Now he has left, serving the wrong god—a victim of himself and his sin. What a tragedy," Jesus lamented. "Unless he changes his mind, he will never taste forgiveness and fellowship with my Father. Does he realize he has set aside his salvation—his chance for real life? What a turnaround. The man came looking for eternal life and walked away from life now and after death."

Jesus was clear about his mission in life. Even before his death and resurrection he was intent on calling people to new life that was eternal. Jesus moved the woman of Samaria to salvation (Jn 4:1-42) fully aware that he was the Messiah and Savior of the world. Whether his invitation was to "believe and follow me" or to "come unto me all you who labor and are broken," Jesus was rescuing people for the kingdom and from themselves.

When someone with the status and wealth of the rich ruler is moving toward the kingdom, our temptation is to bend the rules. Our motives get messed up. We start thinking, "Do you know who I know?" We are attracted to what the conversion of a big-name person will do for our reputations. Leaders of organizations are particularly vulnerable when wealthy, high-profile people show interest in Christ. Money can translate into power and prestige and other dangerous weapons.

Jesus was vulnerable too. If the rich ruler had joined his team, his cause would have been pushed forward. However, his integrity protected him from reducing the cost of commitment. His high regard for truth tempered his desire for results.

Teaching on evangelism is frequently results-oriented. Faithful witnessing is equated with positive results. Sowing is only applauded if there is reaping. This emphasis pressures followers of Jesus to measure their success by counting converts. Guilt results when production figures fall below target quotas. People are viewed as projects rather than full-fledged persons. Friendships are seen only as opportunities to share one's faith. Eventually the motivation to witness is replaced by discouragement. Even those who are well intentioned can be immobilized.

Teaching that focuses on results is also an indictment against Jesus. According to the success criteria, Jesus failed with the rich ruler.

This emphasis on results must be rejected. Jesus' witness is the standard for successful evangelism. His example sets the criteria for all other measurements. Jesus' witness with the rich ruler was successful because it was truthful. Jesus communicated and the rich ruler understood. Faithful witnessing is truth telling, not head counting. The truth stands whether or not it is believed. A negative response does not invalidate the truth or reflect on the faithfulness of the witness.

We witness when we communicate truthfully and people understand. We evangelize when we make God's message clear—just like Jesus did.

2

PREPARING TO WITNESS

H ow can we practice the principles Jesus demonstrated with the rich ruler? Understanding our teacher is one achievement; reproducing his style is another matter. Is it realistic to aim to do so or is his method beyond us? Is his way within our reach?

God has submitted himself to work in partnership with people who will work with him. Followers of Jesus are repeatedly invited to join the drama of drawing other people to God. Without browbeating, the disciples of Christ are simply informed, "You will be my witnesses" (Acts 1:8 RSV). Without resorting to guilt-inducing tactics, Jesus commissions his followers to "go and make disciples" (Mt 28:19 NIV). Without the aid of a suitcase full of promotional gimmicks, those who have been reconciled to God through Christ are given the "ministry of reconciliation" (2 Cor 5:18 RSV).

Reconciling

Reconciliation as an orientation to evangelism is both biblical and right for our times. Broken relationships litter our world. The family is fractured and under attack. Husbands and wives are wounding and leaving each other. Parents and children are at war. Brothers and sisters put each other down. Children blame their parents for their personal problems. Without healing and restoration, the family is doomed.

Society is also under siege. Labor and management push their own interests and often relate as enemies. Various levels of government compete for power. The private sector accuses the public sector of flagrant mismanagement. Church and state take each other to court. Races discriminate against each other. The employed and unemployed, educated and uneducated, rich and poor are polarized. Our society needs bridge builders and peacemakers.

God invites us to join his side and become agents of reconciliation.

Therefore, if any one is in Christ, he is a new creation; the old has passed away, behold, the new has come. All this is from God, who through Christ reconciled us to himself and gave us the ministry of reconciliation; that is, in Christ God was reconciling the world to himself, not counting their trespasses against them, and entrusting to us the message of reconciliation. So we are ambassadors for Christ, God making his appeal through us. We beseech you on behalf of Christ, be reconciled to God. For our sake he made him to be sin who knew no

*sin, so that in him we might become the righteousness
of God. (2 Cor 5:17-21 RSV)*

This passage tells us, first, that reconciliation with the
Father is through Christ. God creates us to be in relationship with himself. He wants us to fulfill his good purposes.
However, we have our own ideas of what is good. We prefer
our sinful ways to God's ways. We persist in writing our own
agendas. God's influence is unwanted. We press for separation from him. God is grieved.

Our disposition to reject God has been the human pattern since Adam and Eve. God's solution was to step into
history and invite us back into rapport with himself. Jesus
Christ was sent to planet Earth. He showed us how to live.
He died so our sin could be dealt with on God's terms. Our
response to Christ's initiative is our way back into relationship with the Father. God is the architect of the entire plan.
He makes all the moves and pays all the costs. We are only
the recipients.

The apostle Paul accepted reconciliation with God
through Christ. And he tells us that those who are reconciled are also assigned the ministry of reconciliation. When
we respond to what God has done through Christ, we are
not only reconciled with the Father, we are new people. We
are changed. Our motives and attitudes are different. Our
ways of thinking and behaving are altered. We are in Christ
and the spirit of Christ is in us.

Our union with God reorders our existence. What God
holds to be good, we hold to be good. His ways become our
ways. His views become our views. We rewrite our agendas
with God's priorities at the top of the list.

We quickly understand that the purpose of Christ's life
and death needs to be known. Just as we need to be reconciled and receive new life in Christ, people around us have

the same need. God's strategy is clear. The reconciled ones are commanded to help others move toward reconciliation with the Father and on to reconciliation with each other.

The redemptive intention of God for his creation is embodied in the spirit of reconciliation. God's aim is to bring healing and wholeness into life. Harmony between himself and his creation is his desire. God is against alienation in his world. He wants peace and unity.

Christians know that the only hope for peace and unity in the world is for individuals to correct their relationship with the God who has created them. There is no personal peace until we have signed our peace treaties with God. There is no unity between us until we are able to see each other with the eyes Christ gives us. Our message is direct. As ambassadors for Christ, our appeal is non-negotiable, "We beseech you on behalf of Christ, be reconciled to God" (v. 20). Our personal touch is persuasive. We come alongside people God sends our way, and we say: "Join me in the family of God."

Although God's game plan may be surprising, he has chosen to communicate his good news in partnership with human messengers. And because Jesus is our example and master teacher, he invites us to reproduce his manner and method. Our witnessing, disciple making and ministry of reconciliation can be "according to Jesus."

Preparing Ourselves
We don't know much about Jesus' life prior to his public ministry. The New Testament is silent about the years between his childhood visit to the temple in Jerusalem and his grueling temptation in the desert. There is nothing in the Scriptures to indicate he organized neighborhood Bible studies in order to get experience. Neither is there evidence

that he attended seminars on how to evangelize. What we know is that his heavenly Father and he were close. Their relationship was intimate. Communication was no problem for them. One overriding condition ruled their relationship: Jesus was anxious to do his Father's will.

Most fundamental in our preparation to share God's good news is our relationship with the Father and his Son. According to God's logic, *we cannot be reconcilers for him until we have first been reconciled to him* (2 Cor 5:18-19). Before we can be partners with God in calling others to believe and repent, we must be new creations in Christ. If our desire is to be God's agents in de-escalating the wars other people are fighting with him, we must have already signed our own peace treaty.

Just as signing a peace treaty and honoring the conditions outlined are two distinct issues, beginning a relationship with Christ and maintaining that relationship are also separate matters. Life with Christ can be like a lapsed friendship—dormant, cold and without current significance. Or, life with Christ can be like a romance on the move—vital, warm and crucial for existence.

A relationship with Christ which lacks current significance is not a relationship, it is a historical event. The Scriptures teach we are compelled by Christ's love to persuade men to believe (2 Cor 5:11, 14). If our lives are not embraced by Christ and our wills submitted to his wishes, our witness will not only be absent, it will be negative.

Jesus Christ as Lord and ourselves as his servants (2 Cor 4:5) is what we preach and seek to live. The overriding condition of our relationship is to honor his lordship. And flowing out of our surrender will come his life through us. How else can we be like him?

When it comes to the appropriateness and effectiveness

of our witness, we can be sure of this: more critical than our past experience or the number of evangelism seminars we attend or lead will be the current state of our relationship with our Savior and Lord.

A second crucial element will be *the surety of our faith.* If we are going to publicly confess our faith, sooner or later that faith is going to be challenged. A friend of mine was confronted one day in the chemistry lab. Dave had previously talked about God with a fellow medical student. Thus, he was surprised when his friend said accusingly, "Dave, I had a long conversation with our prof this weekend and we concluded that all you religious people are psychologically sick."

Dave's immediate reaction was to lash back with a verbal insult. Then he thought a more refined approach would be to acknowledge every person's right to be wrong. God must have controlled his caustic tongue because when he spoke, he lifted his head so his eyes would meet his friend's, and he took the bait that had been offered: "So you think I'm psychologically sick. Go ahead. Support your charge."

How would you have handled that incident? What would be your strategy in the discussion that followed? If Jesus had been faced with that predicament, what do you think he would have done?

If you suffer from the disease of "Christian Apologitis," the accusation would inflict mental and verbal paralysis. Your first reaction might have been to hope no one else heard the charge so you would be protected from further embarrassment. Later—like sometime the next day—you would have thought of a clever comeback.

If, on the other hand, you have reasonable confidence in what and why you believe, after the initial shock waves had subsided, you might have welcomed the challenge. Your response undoubtedly would have been different from Dave's, but you would not have closed the door on the opportunity to extend the discussion. You eventually might have used the situation to turn the focus of the conversation to what your friend believed.

Knowing what and why you believe does not guarantee personal security or become a substitute for social skills. Neither does being able to articulate and defend your faith mean that all questions asked will have satisfactory answers. The Bible does not speak to all issues. Some concerns, such as the problem of suffering, do not have complete answers. We are still looking through a glass darkly (1 Cor 13:12) and must be honest about our darkness as well as our light. As John Stott suggested, we do well to guard our integrity and hold our unresolved problems in a "suspense account."

On the other hand, knowing what and why you believe is part of the equipment needed to prepare you as God's messenger. Reading and thinking about what you believe builds your faith. Studying and discussing why you believe with other Christians injects both conviction and confidence. Praying and struggling over some of the hard questions will give substance to your claim to believe and provide a basis for self-respect. You will be "prepared to make a defense to any one who calls you to account for the hope that is in you . . . with gentleness and reverence" (1 Pet 3:15 RSV).

In addition to being prepared to express and defend our faith, to be effective witnesses we ought to *pray for people around us.* During his active ministry, Jesus developed a reputation as someone who prayed (see Mk 1:35; Jn 17). In our pursuit of a Christlike life and our commitment to communicate with people as he did, we will aim at the same reputation.

Personal and corporate prayer is a declaration of our dependence on God. The posture of prayer is one of submission. As we surrender ourselves to God, he embraces us. And in some mysterious but undeniable fashion, he makes our weakness strong (2 Cor 12:9).

Prayer confirms our working relationship with the Holy Spirit in our ministry of witness and reconciliation. We are to complement what God is already doing in those he wants to bring to himself. We know that God has reserved for himself the responsibility of convicting people of their sin (Jn 16:8-11). We are assigned to speak the truth in love (Eph 4:15) and to be salt and light in our people worlds (Mt 5:13-16 and Lk 13:21). Prayer unites us with God in our shared mission.

Praying for the people who share our lives heightens our awareness of them. We pray for roommates and neighbors —by name. We pray for colleagues and lab partners. In order that we will not be silent when we should speak, we ask our heavenly Father to help us understand what our friends believe and where they are in their relationship with him. We pray that we will recognize lonely people in crowded cafeterias and risk inviting ourselves to share their table. We pray for friends and members of our families and for the individuals we don't naturally like but who keep hanging around us. We pray that we will speak with care and act as Jesus would around such people. Asking that they may be open to being taught God's truth, we pray for those who teach us or those we teach. We pray for the people at work—those who work under us and those under whom we work. We make lists of the people who share our lives and pray for our ministry of reconciliation among them.

But we also pray for ourselves . . . that we will be released from excessive preoccupation with ourselves so we can really listen to others. We pray that God will help us overcome our fears of being rejected and of being thought by others to be "too religious." We pray that we will both see and make opportunities to love and witness appropriately.

Finally, we pray for our fellow believers who are committed to sharing the faith. In order to pray intelligently for each other, we enter into prayer covenants with them and exchange prayer lists. We pray that we will be faithful. We pray that we will be used by God to nudge people around us toward new life in Christ. We pray, and in humility before God, we confess that when it comes to prayer, we are learners. So we also ask the Lord to "teach us to pray" (Lk 11:1 RSV).

3

APPLYING
THE MIND
OF CHRIST

*U*nderstanding the Christian faith and the scope of God's truth is like putting together a seven-hundred-piece jigsaw puzzle. Each piece is equivalent to a component of God's truth. Each piece exists as a simple entity but has significance only when it is interlocked with other pieces. Each piece has a place in the whole, but without each piece in its proper place, the picture is incomplete.

Our aim should be to put God's picture of truth together. As we grow up in Christ, we put more pieces in their right places. The limits of our humanity and the incompleteness of life this side of heaven preclude putting all seven hundred pieces together. Perfection is beyond our reach in this life even though we are in Christ. However, there will be a correlation between the completeness of the picture and our perception of the artist and his hopes for all his creation.

Christians who operate with too few pieces of the truth puzzle are vulnerable to excesses and can become easy victims of half-truths. They often cannot adequately distinguish their Christian faith from other beliefs, and they are at a loss to defend their faith from attack. Such people can be attracted by cults which call themselves Christian but which differ in subtle but critical areas.

Other Christians try to theorize their way into the kingdom of heaven. They live out their faith by searching for the missing pieces of the truth puzzle. They cling to the study table of learning and never quite make it to the playing field of life.

The Christian Mind

In trying to put on the mind of Christ we must first be sure that what we believe is *accurate*. In God's picture, the meaning of John 3:16-18 must be kept at the center of the puzzle.

> *For God so loved the world that he gave his one and only Son, that whoever believes in him shall not perish but have eternal life. For God did not send his Son into the world to condemn the world, but to save the world through him. Whoever believes in him is not condemned, but whoever does not believe stands condemned already because he has not believed in the name of God's one and only Son. (NIV)*

The cross and the empty tomb are the crux of our faith. God's love for a broken and sinning creation needs to be repeated frequently. The puzzle cannot be put together unless we know that Jesus Christ gave his life to be the Savior of the world. But our puzzle picture is incomplete if we reduce the truth to only those pieces.

Beyond being accurate, our belief must also be *comprehensive.* The central pieces of God's truth must not be isolated from the other pieces. You can't reduce the size of the puzzle to make it easier to comprehend. Christian truth infringes on all areas of life. For instance, God's Word in 1 John 3:16-18 is also a part of our puzzle:

This is how we know what love is: Jesus Christ laid down his life for us. And we ought to lay down our lives for our brothers. If anyone has material possessions and sees his brother in need but has no pity on him, how can the love of God be in him? Dear children, let us not love with words or tongue but with actions and in truth. (NIV)

Christian truth touches economics as well as ecclesiology, politics as well as prayer.

Before Jesus launched his public ministry, he took time to put the pieces of God's truth puzzle together. His mind was not idle as he sanded tables in the carpenter shop. He was processing his thoughts and refining his thinking. His later articulation of truth did not flow out of a vacuum. As a result of his preparation he was ready to speak the truth regardless of the subject matter. As we have already noted, his witness was frequently framed within the context and focused on the content of the moment. Jesus was always reading the present situation. We can admire his mental maneuvers.

When the question was posed, "Is it right to pay taxes to Caesar?" Jesus asked for a coin and created time to ponder his answer. Holding the coin so his audience could see Caesar's inscription, he asked, "Whose portrait in this?"

"Caesar's," they replied.

Jesus drew the bottom line: "Give to Caesar what is Caesar's and to God what is God's (Mk 12:17 NIV). Jesus allowed his Father's truth to penetrate all that he thought and did. He had an integrated view of his whole life.

Our tendency is to keep God out of a lot of life. He is often restricted to what we categorize as being spiritual. "God: do not enter" signs are posted in our minds when we read the sports page, shop for groceries or study educational learning theories. We make more room for God in Bible studies, worship services and discussions on ethics and morality. Os Guinness attributes our divorcing God from much of life to the "eclipse of the Christian mind." If we want to practice Jesus' way of evangelizing, we must develop minds that are distinctly and holistically Christian.

The Scriptures speak with clarity about the place of the mind in the Christian life. A changed and renewed mental perspective is an intrinsic part of becoming a new Christian. The following references illustrate this (italics throughout are mine):

☐ Ephesians 4:22-24: "Put off your old nature which belongs to your former manner of life and is corrupt through deceitful lusts, *and be renewed in the spirit of your minds,* and put on the new nature, created after the likeness of God in true righteousness and holiness." (RSV)

☐ Romans 12:2: "Do not be conformed to this world but *be transformed by the renewal of your mind,* that you may prove what is the will of God." (RSV)

People who are in Christ are to have the mind of Christ. Their minds are to be renovated. Their thought processes are to be reprogrammed.

☐ 1 Corinthians 2:16: " 'For who has known the mind of the Lord so as to instruct him?' But *we have the mind of Christ."* (RSV)

An awake Christian mind is to act as a sorting device and a warning system for followers of Jesus.

□ Colossians 2:8: "See to it that no one makes prey of you by philosophy and empty deceit, according to human tradition, according to the elemental spirits of the universe, and not *according to Christ."* (RSV)

The mind is also to be used to think as Jesus thought, to understand as he understood.

□ 1 Peter 4:1: "Since therefore Christ suffered in the flesh, *arm yourselves with the same thought."* (RSV)

The mind is part of the whole person who is invited to know and love God.

□ Mark 12:30: "You shall love the Lord your God with all your heart, and with all your soul, and *with all your mind,* and with all your strength." (RSV)

Harry Blamires has written a profound book called *The Christian Mind.* The book revolves around three helpful assumptions:

a. Our Christian mind is built an an informed awareness of what a Christian believes, what Jesus teaches and the Scriptures declare. With it we can filter and measure data within a Christian frame of reference.

b. Whether the data is political or economic, whether the subject matter is historical or contemporary, whether the issue is justice or Jesus, our awake Christian mind leads to clear Christian thinking.

c. Distinct Christian thinking then becomes the basis for right Christian choice and behavior.

Developing a Christian mind is not an option; it is a necessity. Christian thinking is not restricted to brainy people. The ability to think is a reflection of creation in the image of God, and the call to think "Christianly" is the consequence of re-creation in the image of Christ. Disregarding the place of the mind will lead to half-life Christianity. Without an operating Christian mind, we will either separate our faith from the affairs of the world or surrender to the secular squeeze of society.

Our world is a pagan place where God is not in charge. Isaiah's warning still stands:

"My thoughts are not your thoughts,
neither are your ways my ways," declares the LORD. (Is 55:8-9 NIV)

A Christian student at a secular university will likely be taught sociology from a Marxist perspective and psychology with a deterministic flavor. Economics may be propped up with capitalistic premises, philosophy with pragmatic biases, biology with evolutionary presuppositions and the other sciences with natural-law limitations. A day could well start with a course in religious studies taught by a self-confessed atheist and conclude with a date to a dorm party that turns into a "boozefest."

Our society is built on these same foundations and is potentially harmful to our spiritual health. Advertisers stalk us like big-game hunters on a safari. Selfishness is paraded as virtuous. Messages massage our minds and appeal to our senses to "believe in me, experience me, flirt with me, touch me, caress me, give yourself to me." Without God's protection and our Christian minds, we will be seduced by the spirit of our age.

As you develop your Christian mind, thinking will be a regular part of your day. A search for God's truth will be on the agenda. Thoughtfulness will be a comfortable posture. Your commitment to think your way through life will merge God's understanding with your own. The "God: do not enter" signs will be scrapped. You will invite God into all departments of life. And, if you choose, the framework for your witness will expand. Random conversations will open up doors to communicate naturally. Existing relationships will offer a ready-made context to tell the truth from God's point of view. Opportunities for a life-centered witness will multiply.

You will go to classes, weighing in your mind the contrast between what your psychology prof will propose about existing as a human being and what the Scriptures teach. You may speak out or ask a question.

You will drive by a billboard and be invited to believe the slogan, "You can change your life at the spa." Your Christian mind will react. You reject the notion that your quality of life will change significantly by reducing the size of your waist. You may take initiative toward your passenger by asking, "What do you think about that claim?"

You will hear oil-rich governments defend their pricing policies so they can add to their bulging trust funds, and you will smell the foul odor of selfishness. You will be offended, write protest letters and (if the opportunity arises) confront cabinet ministers over lunch.

You will read books that tell you to assert yourself, "pull your own strings" and "take care of number one." The caution flag will come out because you know God tells you to "do nothing from selfishness or conceit, but in humility count others better than yourselves" (Phil 2:3 RSV). You will express concern, even risk rejection, when others around you live and push the new gospel of self.

You will watch television and be forced to filter the claims of commercials. You will be attracted by the pleasant music and lyrics of the jingle: "Get those things that really count. Just say 'charge it' on your Sears account." But you will resist the message and the manipulation. You know the things that really count in life are not purchased on your charge card. You will remember God's warning to be sure "no one takes you captive through hollow and deceptive philosophy, which depends on human tradition and the basic principles of this world rather than on Christ" (Col 2:8 NIV).

Your attention will be grabbed by a movie review: "A delightful romantic romp about a couple who work, love and live compatibly—until they wreck a good relationship by getting married." You will invite a friend or neighbor to go with you to see the movie and then enjoy coffee and dessert. You know ahead of time that you will have difficulty not getting into a conversation about marriage. There will be ample opportunity to reflect on God's hopes and dreams for family life.

You will listen to a husband and wife harass each other and sense deep hatred between them. You will understand their need to experience forgiveness in order for them to have a future together. Your counsel will point them to our forgiving God who will give them the power to forgive each other.

You will applaud believers like Malcolm Muggeridge, a former world-roaming journalist, for thinking and speaking Christianly. During an interview, he was asked about the value of travel and replied, "The founder of the Christian religion never travelled more than thirty miles and associated with what we would class as uninteresting people. If he had been given a package tour of the Roman Empire and had the pleasure of meeting a selection of officials, writers and eminent people, I doubt that the New Testament would be more profound." What an intriguing way to witness creatively.

In the past, I became troubled by some political develop-

ments in Canada. Our federal attorney general and chief
minister of justice committed an apparent criminal act.
He allegedly forged the signature of his lover's husband in
order to process the abortion of his illicit child. When the
apparent act became public, the attorney general resigned
his cabinet position but continued to sit as an elected member of Parliament. Although forgery is a violation of the
criminal code, another politician decided not to prosecute.
The embarrassment suffered and the cabinet resignation
were cited as sufficient punishment to assure justice. While
commenting on the incident, the prime minister indicated
that the door was open for the former attorney general to
assume another position in the cabinet at some future time.

From a biblical point of view, I was disturbed that the
prime minister was ready to assign a position of leadership
with status and power to an individual who apparently
lacked moral and legal integrity (1 Tim 3:1-7). I expressed
my dissent to a group of friends who reminded me that the
prime minister was going to be in our city that night for a
forum and political rally. They suggested I voice my dis-
approval to him personally. They put teeth in the idea by
offering to go with me.

My sense of security was much less intact that night
when I stood before the microphone in front of several
thousand people and blinding television lights. After sum-
marizing the events surrounding the former attorney general's resignation and pointing out the prime minister's
readiness to offer another cabinet post, I asked, "What is
your view on the relationship between personal morality
and the right to hold high public office? Mr. Prime Minister, what does a person have to do to disqualify himself as
a potential member of your cabinet?"

The prime minister paused and then began to talk about

forgiveness and his reticence to be judgmental. The crowd clapped and screamed their approval of his remarks. I felt intimidated and very alone but still right about posing the question. The next day, several newspapers isolated the questions and responded to the issues raised. To my knowledge, no one became a believer because of that encounter, but a Christian concern was expressed.

Activating our Christian mind will allow us to tell the truth from God's point of view about anything and everything. Expanding our witness to thoughtful truth telling will multiply our opportunities to think clearly and speak appropriately. Whether the subject is travel, nuclear warfare, clothing styles, sports, entertainment, work, life or death—we can tune into the conversation and speak on target. Whether a person is facing the future with confidence or fear, swamped with past failures, solving a present problem, expressing a value judgment or musing about God or money, our response can connect with the individual's current interest or concern.

The content of our Christian witness is broader than Jesus' giving himself for the sins of the world. We need to think and speak "Christianly" about our use of the environment and leisure, the consequences of what people believe and do, matters of global disparity, pornography, sexual exploitation, depersonalization and television.

Bringing God's perspective to an issue is faithful witnessing. Sowing seeds of truth is honest evangelism. As we learn to apply the mind of Christ to all of life, we will find increased opportunities to appropriately share our faithful witness. We will also discover that because the teachings of Jesus and Scripture are our authority when offering a Christian perspective, the step to dealing directly with Jesus and the significance of the cross is a short one.

Understanding the Beliefs of Others

After I spoke at a university campus on the subject "Is Believing Christianity Intellectual Suicide?" two young men expressed disagreement with my position. The cafeteria was nearby, so I invited them for coffee and a discussion. I attempted to give reasons for the faith and hope that is in me (1 Pet 3:15). My approach was to diagram the Christian position and support the claims of God's existence, Christ's historical presence and resurrection, the credibility of the Scriptures and the validity of my experience. My two new friends delighted in pointing out gaps in my belief system and suggesting I had problems. In the midst of our sparring match, the time arrived to turn the tables. I reached for a piece of paper and asked both young men to diagram for me what they believed. Initially they were stunned by the idea, but eventually they picked up their pens and put their keen minds to work. During the next half-hour we discussed their belief systems. Then it was my turn to delight in pointing out the gaps in their beliefs.

Believing is like breathing. If we are alive, we do it. Everyone's belief system may not be clearly defined or even consciously chosen but it exists. Everyone believes something and operates with a framework that tries to make sense of life through assumptions, values and personal priorities. *Relating to people who are not Christians requires an understanding of what beliefs they hold.* G. K. Chesterton once said: "When people stop believing in God, it is assumed that they believe in nothing. But it is far worse than that—because then they believe in anything."

When we lowered our microscopes on Jesus' life and style of witness, we saw him giving careful attention to his audience. He was concerned to understand other people. He did not deliver predetermined messages, but responded to people based on his reading the pulse beat of what they believed and wanted to talk about. His communication consistently connected with people's needs because he was released from himself and free to focus on others.

The apostle Paul practiced the same principles. He showed the inevitability of belief when he addressed the philosophers on Mars Hill and announced, "Men of Athens, I perceive that in every way you are very religious. For as I passed along, and observed the objects of your worship, I found also an altar with this inscription, 'To an unknown god' " (Acts 17:22-23 RSV). Paul quoted from his listeners' prophets. What Paul understood about the men of Athens provided the springboard to present what he believed about creation and Christ's resurrection.

Everyone embraces a world view and surrenders himself or herself to some belief. Recognizing this, we can see the necessity to turn from our preoccupation with telling what we believe to a determination to discover what others believe. Like Jesus and Paul, once we get inside another person's frame of reference, we will be able to connect our communication to his or her world on the way to building bridges to our own.

If more effective communication flows out of understanding what other people believe, a release from defensiveness springs from realizing that *whatever people believe, they believe by faith.* Science extols the idea that if you cannot prove your premise in a test tube, your claim is suspect. The inability to prove God's existence in test-tube terms has intimidated many of God's people. The mere idea of pleading "guilty" to faith generates defensiveness and feelings of inferiority. But feeling apologetic about living by faith is completely unnecessary.

Everyone lives by faith, regardless of what he or she believes. There are no exceptions. The materialist who believes the best life is found by accumulating money and piling up as many perishables as possible lives by faith. Materialists stake their lives on what cannot be proved. Scientists live by faith in the presuppositions of science. Humanists who limit their calculations in life to their own resources live by faith in their assumptions. Committed pleasure seekers, convinced existentialists and success-driven secularists all live by faith.

I welcome those rare occasions to talk with thinking atheists. If the situation permits, I delight in challenging them with statements like, "The one thing I admire about you is your faith. Frankly, you have more faith than I do. From my view of the evidence, it takes more faith to conclude that God does not exist than it does to risk your life on the claim of his existence."

But even though there is ample evidence to support the Christian claims, in the parable of the Sower (Mt 13:1-9) Jesus warns us to expect Christian wipeouts. We will find little reason to celebrate when only one out of four seeds grows permanently and produces fruit.

Several years ago, on a frozen January morning, a letter arrived from a friend who was also an Inter-Varsity student leader. I still hurt inside when I read the message.

Wednesday morning
January 23

Dear Don,

I cannot lose God and I cannot find him. I am wrenched apart by not being able to believe and feeling myself damned for my unbelief. For some time, I have peeled away the layers of my belief, thinking that I was discarding everything extraneous to leave a strong, elemental nut of faith. But now when I get to it, I find there is noth-

ing there. God knows I know what solace there is in belief, but I cannot believe.

What a tragic statement. Movement away from God is always regrettable. I must assert, however, that movement
from God is always movement toward belief in something
else. To opt out of Christian faith forces one to opt for another faith. Confronting wavering Christians with the re-
ality that giving up their Christian belief leads them to embrace another form of faith may help trigger renewed commitment to Christ.

Pressing people about what they believe and why they
believe as they do is good strategy. Paul's theology of evangelism and witness includes opening the eyes of unbeliev-
ers and turning them from "darkness to light and from the
power of Satan to God, that they may receive forgiveness of
sins and a place among those who are sanctified by faith in
[Christ]" (Acts 26:18 RSV). Opening people's eyes to the
inadequacies of their own belief positions will encourage
them to consider other alternatives, including Christ and
his claims.

We must not, however, develop a judgmental spirit toward what others believe. An attitude of superiority will
close eyes rather than open them. Jesus is our model again.
He did not force people to accept him. God refuses to coerce
people to believe and live as he wishes. Therefore, we must
extend to them the same freedom.

People usually make contact with God in the same way
we screw a light bulb into an electrical socket . . . step by
step and stage by stage. We turn the bulb a little at a time,
until contact is made and the light goes on. People are
normally prompted to turn their attention toward God in
the same gradual manner. They are nudged and prodded
by God and circumstances, again and again, until contact

is made and Christ's forgiveness and love light up their lives.

In the physical realm, we easily observe the patterns of change from baby to child and from adolescent to adult. Psychologists tell us that we also develop cognitively and emotionally through identifiable and predictable stages. In the moral department, we may argue with Kohlberg and his theories, but we are forced to conclude that there is also a process of moral maturing.

This pattern of progressive human change also applies in the spiritual realm. Most people start the process by concluding that God exists. Their development then moves them:

☐ to accept the basics of the gospel,

☐ to believe Jesus' historical death has personal significance,

☐ to admit their personal needs, and

☐ then to confess and repent and place their faith in Christ.

This is why Paul could observe, "I planted the seed, Apollos watered it, but God made it grow" (1 Cor 3:6 NIV). Philippians 1:6 delivers the same message: "He who began a good work in you will carry it on to completion until the day of Christ Jesus" (NIV).

When we view the movement toward God as a developmental process we are not trying to make everyone's experience uniform. Some people skip stages and take giant leaps toward God. By emphasizing the process of conversion, we are not attempting to produce another mold to bring God under our control. Instead, our object is to raise our awareness that different individuals are at different stages in the process of spiritual perception and decision making. God by his Spirit uses different people, means and methods to nudge others along toward himself.

Consequently, we should try to speak to people where they are in their spiritual development. Attempting to convince people that Jesus is God and his death has personal significance is premature if they are honestly questioning whether God exists. Encouraging people to repent and place their faith in Christ when they have no sense of personal need is futile—and possibly detrimental.

We need to be honest. Most people are not ready to receive Christ as their Savior. They are a few steps away from that life-changing experience. Sensitive witnesses will assist seekers to walk toward the embrace of Christ; they will relate to people where they are and answer the questions that are being asked. If questions aren't being asked, we can try to start the questioning process.

As we seek to personalize God's truth in this manner, we are forced to give up using gospel packages. The "one message" approach for all people in every situation cannot possibly apply to the diversity of human circumstances. Every culture has distinctive markings. People come in different shapes and sizes. Each individual is unique. Cloning is not God's way, and neither should it be ours. Reducing our witness to a stereotyped method is like asking all people to wear the same size and style of clothing. God specializes in tailor-made suits, and we are his tailors.

Christians, too, come in all shapes and sizes. Because we are not all alike, we can minister to people of varying sorts. God has a network of people representing him. He moves in and out of the lives of non-Christians through his body of believers. It is our privilege to link arms with each other in the sequence of events that help people move toward God. Like Paul and Apollos, we can be servants through whom others come to believe (1 Cor 3:5).

4

COMMUNICATING THE GOSPEL

*F*or many Christians the thought of witnessing is like pulling the trigger on a big, old shotgun. The emotional kickback is paralyzing. Many of God's people react in a manner that's a long way from Jesus' image of fishing in a quiet stream.

During a planning session with students, one admission led to another:

"Our group is big, but not very good at evangelizing," Dave revealed.

"Our motif for evangelizing is—by accident only," said Sue.

Everyone in the circle was jarred by Jim's honesty: "I

haven't witnessed for months."

Julie lamented, "I'm not cutting it with my peers. My classmates don't even know I'm a Christian."

Elaine announced, her voice breaking, "I'm a new Christian. I have non-Christian friends. I am involved with them. But I don't know what to say or how to say it. Please help me. . . ."

Most of us feel inadequate when it comes to witnessing. We know we don't do it enough, or we don't do it well. We are afraid of failure, and we don't know where to begin. In this chapter I want to offer six practical suggestions for reaching out to others.

1. Be an Attentive Listener

Many of God's people limit witnessing to talking. Their one-track delivery system consists of getting the message out, speaking the right words and telling the truth. Whether people really hear the message is secondary to the gospel's being proclaimed. This style of witness treats individuals like a radio audience.

To be an effective communicator of God's good news, you should be an attentive listener. You should give yourself to the people who speak to you. Jesus' commitment to listen was rooted in his high regard for people. You need that same regard. Because people are important, what they are saying matters and is worth trying to understand. Instead of pretending you grasp everything, as a good listener you will ask questions, such as: "Am I correct in what I hear you saying . . . ?"

Good listeners are also good watchers, picking up non-verbal signals that amplify certain concerns. Good listeners resist the urge to communicate a sense of superiority. Instead of thinking about our brilliant responses, we will listen to what is being said. Looking people in the eyes communicates, "I hear you!" But looking at a watch sends the message, "I'm too busy for you." Continually changing the subject transmits the signal, "You bore me."

In our fallen nature, we often tend to equate pretty faces and pleasing personalities with personal worth and the ability to think and speak intelligently. But a good listener will not make that assumption.

Jesus was a good listener. He knew that attentive listening had to precede talk that was true and on target. In his personal discussions he had a way of hearing what was important and then dealing with what mattered (Mk 10:17-22). When his audience asked him questions, his ears and eyes heard them accurately, and then he spoke succinctly with his mind and his lips (Lk 20:21-25). We can be equipped to be like our Lord.

2. Take Initiative

Some time ago, I had one of those divine encounters on a commuter flight coming home from a weekend retreat. I was tired and hoping for solitude, but the cabin was crowded so I reluctantly shifted to the middle seat. A young woman asked if she could sit in the empty place next to me. She was a self-assured, briefcase-carrying, glamorous woman. We talked through the preliminaries about where we were going and what our work was, and we exchanged first names. Susan turned out to be a sales representative on her way up the organizational ladder.

Sensing her aura of self-confidence, I played a hunch and asked if she had been exposed to some of the current "Self-Assertiveness Training" seminars. She came back with an affirmative smile and said how important it was to be in control of one's life. I countered that I wasn't sure we were strong enough to pull that off in a world that so power-fully tries to control us. We talked about where we get our personal resources.

At one point in the conversation, Susan dropped a hint that God had a part in her life. I asked her if she was a fol-lower of Jesus. She smiled again and said she was a new be-liever. In the next few minutes, Susan dropped her over-confident disguise and we talked about real life—worry for her unbelieving but spiritually open husband, concerns about her kids, confusion about her life, her personal strug-gles and on and on.

The next morning, I wrote a friend who lives in Susan's community and told him about our conversation. I sug-gested Susan was a healthy mix between her work, the human-potential movement and Jesus, and she needed to be discipled. "By chance," my friend just happened to know her husband. The contact resulted in the two couples start-ing a Bible study together.

The Inter-Varsity group at the University of Alberta con-cluded that God wanted more to happen through them on their campus. They decided to hold each other accountable to invite a non-Christian friend to an evening discussion of the topic, "What Is a Christian?" Ernie was president of the group, and he prayerfully decided to approach a classmate. The perfect moment to make the invitation never seemed to arrive. Finally, he blurted out, "Jim, you know that I am a Christian. A group of us are inviting a few friends over next week to discuss the question, 'What Is a Christian?' Would you come with me?"

Jim was not prepared to accept the invitation. He lashed back at Ernie. "Listen, I count you as one of my friends but if you push that religious stuff at me, you won't be for long!!"

Ernie kept his cool. He responded to Jim's hostility by trying to find its root. "Jim, you surprise me. Why is the religious issue such an emotional one for you?"

Jim must have seen himself in a mirror because he responded to Ernie's comeback with the suggestion that they go for coffee and an explanation. They spent the next hour discussing Jim's heavy religious background and why he had turned away from God.

"Too aggressive!" Is that your reaction? You want to go back to more theory about Jesus' approach? "Let's face facts," you say. "Most people don't feel like taking that kind of initiative. Steering conversations so they deal with real substance takes foresight and energy. Our society specializes in superficiality, not substance. Turning the corner in conversations to include spiritual matters raises the risk of rejection. Anyway, where do we get the prerogative to intrude into other people's private space?"

Thanks for the interruption. That's exactly how I feel. But then again, that's just the point, isn't it? Honoring the lordship of Christ isn't something we do at the level of feelings. Jesus didn't promise, "Follow me and you'll feel good." His mandate is to a higher calling. According to our Lord, we are the salt of the earth and the light of the world. We have been instructed by the Son of God to make disciples. We have Jesus' example of touching people's control centers. We are to express our ministry of reconciliation and witness in his name whether we feel like it or not. That is our prerogative. If we are still worried about risk and rejection, we need to remember that Jesus was crucified.

So, we will take initiative. We will plan neighborhood video parties. We will invite friends from our faculties or work places to see and discuss current films. Our film selections will raise issues and make social statements that stimulate discussion. Our options could include

☐ Chariots of Fire
☐ Whose Life Is It Anyway?
☐ Ordinary People
☐ Kramer vs. Kramer
☐ If You Love This Planet
☐ The Chosen
☐ Tootsie
☐ Gandhi

3. Ask Questions That Matter

Thoughtful questions open doors to quality conversations. In soliciting information and opinions from people, we gather data that allows us to understand and relate to them. Someone ends up directing conversations, and those who ask the questions most often determine the direction.

But there are dangers. Honest inquiry can lead to skillful manipulation. Asking questions can become a role to be played rather than an honest expression of interest in people. Like other good things, asking questions, even to express love and truth, can be abused. Potential abuse, however, does not preclude careful use. The idea is not to dominate or control but to ask questions that encourage people to state who they are and what they think. With that information, you can make an appropriate response.

Philip was sent by God on an evangelistic assignment to the desert outside Jerusalem (Acts 8). He was to contact an Ethiopian eunuch. He found the man riding in his carriage and reading from the book of Isaiah. Philip's use of the question was simple but brilliant. He asked, "Do you understand what you are reading?" Within fifteen seconds, the two men were having a Bible study together.

I was invited to an awards banquet as a guest of some

students. I was looking for a place to sit and praying for significant conversation. I moved toward an opening and introduced myself to an unconventional-looking guy named Wolfgang. He was graduating in a couple of months with a degree in education, so the natural question was, "Have you found a job? Does anyone in the world out there want you?"

His answer was a little surprising: "I'm going to South America to lie on the beaches for a year or two."

My comeback was, "Why have you bothered with university? What do you believe life is about anyway?"

For the next five minutes, Wolfgang made his defenses. Toward the end of his musings, he dropped the comment that he believed in reincarnation.

With interest, I observed that "in one sense, I believe in reincarnation too."

Wolfgang was intrigued enough to ask, "What do you mean?"

I explained that I was a follower of Jesus and that meant I was attempting to re-incarnate the life Jesus had already demonstrated. We spent the rest of the meal chewing on that idea.

Questions are like the banks of a river; they channel the flow of the conversation. They can be a means of helping people discover what they think and believe. Sequence questions will often press people to deal with the logical consequences of what they just said. How often have we heard someone glibly announce, "Of course I believe in God." The pursuing question, "How does your belief in God affect your behavior?" deals with the claim at a more significant level.

As well as being a tool for transmitting God's good news, the tactful use of questions is an invaluable social skill—but only when interest is genuine. A double-barreled warning should be fired with each question: Don't ask unless you really want to know, and don't ask unless you are committed to listen.

The Scriptures inform us that at the age of twelve, Jesus was in the temple "sitting among the teachers, listening to them and asking them questions" (Lk 2:46 RSV). (By the way, his parents were not impressed.) Even a casual reading of the Gospels will reveal that Jesus continued to hone both his listening and questioning skills. Surely the whole spirit of the gospel is epitomized in Jesus' open-ended question to the paralytic, "Do you want to be healed?" (Jn 5:6 RSV). We sense a cutting edge for the gospel revolving around the question Jesus repeated about himself, "Who do you say that I am?" (Mk 8:29 RSV).

4. State a Biblical Plan of Salvation

Jesus was ready to make an issue of his own identity because he knew he was the Son of God who had come to be the Savior of the world. The danger of encouraging a style of witness that offers Christian perspectives on various issues is that the most crucial issue of Jesus' identity and his ultimate purpose can be neglected. We know from experience that Jesus' claims are exclusive, and many people who face the real Jesus find him offensive. We are more comfortable offering a Christian point of view on abortion or the Middle East than we are pressing the point that Jesus died to redeem us and deserves the position of Lord and Controller of our lives. When we yield to the temptation to remain comfortable, our evangelism will be left at the seeding stage.

On the journey from seeding to reaping, our verbal witness will usually follow three strategic stages. Our conversations will turn corners:

☐ from ordinary talk to spiritual discussions when a distinct Christian point of view is expressed,

☐ from spiritual discussions to Christ-centered content when Jesus is the subject matter, and

☐ from Christ-centered content to an invitation to believe and make a personal commitment to Jesus Christ as Savior and Lord.

In the context of a personal friendship, the process may evolve over a month's time or a number of years. In the instance of a random relationship, one of those divine appointments, the whole process could happen during a single occasion.

If God has one of those special appointments set up for you today, would you recognize the opportunity? Would you be able to concisely state a biblical plan of salvation? Do you have a clear outline of the gospel filed in your mind that you can share now? Would you be able to take your Bible and systematically move from passage to passage? Can you clarify what God has done in Christ? Can you stipulate what God requires for a person to become a Christian believer? After your appointment was over, would you be confident that you had been God's prepared instrument and that the new believer's faith in Christ had a biblical basis?

There are many right ways to present God's plan of salvation. God's activity is not restricted to a set formula or pattern. Rather than being controlled like a programmed computer, the Holy Spirit blows like the wind—when and where the Father wills. But while there are no magic words to chant when helping someone meet Christ, there is specific content to convey. Our role in partnership with the Holy Spirit is to make clear what Christ has done on our behalf.

Numerous plans of salvation have been written and are

readily available. They are helpful to systematically communicate the gospel and to serve as reaping tools. We use them and keep them in their proper place by remembering that the Holy Spirit does the convicting, and the miracle of salvation is a gift of God through Christ. Our role is to supplement what God is doing by communicating the message of what Christ has done, offering our personal presence and guidance, and then confirming the new believer's forgiven status with the Father.

God wants to preserve the uniqueness of our personalities as we assist others to meet Christ. We are not suddenly reduced to robots because we are about to be used in this business of helping someone become a Christian. So, when it comes to plans of salvation, the best plan for many of us is to study the Scriptures and develop our own. Some will link a series of passages together. Others will adopt the parable of the Prodigal Son as a framework. The parable of the Sower and the four kinds of seeds will be helpful to a few (Mt 13:1-23). Some will express their creativity by developing an analogy as a communication vehicle. Falling in love and getting married is one such analogy that can serve to present the gospel. A story about the restoration of a broken friendship or the reconciliation of a married couple can provide a way to tell God's good news about redemption. The universal experience of conception, birth, life and death could be a powerful means of delivering God's plan for life.

The consequences of Christ's death and resurrection can be hooked to a subject like change, reconciliation, forgiveness, truth, belief, values and ethics. Other people might be stimulated to follow Jesus through a discussion that contrasts lust for money, power and sex with freedom in Christ.

Questions like "How are Christians different?" "Where

do we find personal significance?" and "How do we decide what is right and wrong?" can serve as a means of communicating God's plan to rescue his creatures and creation.

Jesus questioned the sick man at the pool, "Do you want to be healed?" (Jn 5:1-11 RSV). That question can open the door to a gospel presentation that revolves around people's needs, linking Jesus and the cross to a battered self-image, the inner ache of failure, personal insecurity, loneliness, rejection or the drive for wholeness. On the other hand, a presentation built around your personal testimony and experience with Christ may be your way to influence people around you.

As the Holy Spirit stimulates us, our privilege is to be creative and truthful at the same time. The following four plans are different in style. One approach may be compatible with your personality and taste.

The human disease. This first plan of salvation uses a disease as an analogy for sin. It includes appropriate biblical references to explain God's plan of salvation to those who have not heard or accepted God's message.

The Problem

1. We choose to sin (Is 53:6; Rom 3:23).
2. Our sin separates us from God (Rom 6:23).
3. We are incomplete apart from God (1 Jn 5:11-13).
4. God desires our fellowship (Rev 3:20).

The Diagnosis

1. Sin is offensive to God (Jn 3:36; Rom 1:18).
2. Sin destroys us and the people around us (Rom 8:6; Eph 4:29-32).
3. God loves us in spite of our sin (Rom 5:8).
4. God sent Christ to resolve the sin problem (Jn 3:16; Eph 2:7-9).

The Cure

1. We must acknowledge our sin and repent of our past (1 Jn 1:9; Lk 5:31-32).

2. We are called to believe in Christ as Savior and Lord (Rom 10:9-10).

3. We are invited to commit our lives to him (Rom 12:1).

The Results

1. We receive the Holy Spirit (Rom 8:9-11).

2. We become members of God's family (Rom 8:15).

3. We change our behavior and seek to please God (Rom 12:2).

4. We experience life with meaning, direction and forgiveness (Jn 10:10; 2 Pet 1:3-4).

5. We receive assurance of eternal life with God (Jn 6:47).

The Prodigal Son. Another approach is to take one of Jesus' parables and build the presentation into the content of the story. Weaving God's plan of salvation around the parable of the Prodigal Son is particularly inviting.

[11]*And he said, "There was a man who had two sons;* [12]*and the younger of them said to his father, 'Father, give me the share of property that falls to me.' And he divided his living between them.* [13]*Not many days later, the younger son gathered all he had and took his journey into a far country, and there he squandered his property in loose living.* [14]*And when he had spent everything, a great famine arose in that country, and he began to be in want.* [15]*So he went and joined himself to one of the citizens of that country, who sent him into his fields to feed swine.* [16]*And he would gladly have fed on the pods that the swine ate; and no one gave him anything.* [17]*But when he came to himself he said, 'How many of my father's hired servants have bread enough and to spare, but I perish here with hunger!* [18]*I will arise and go to my*

father, and I will say to him, "Father, I have sinned against heaven and before you; [19]*I am no longer worthy to be called your son; treat me as one of your hired servants." '* [20]*And he arose and came to his father. But while he was yet at a distance, his father saw him and had compassion, and ran and embraced him and kissed him.* [21]*And the son said to him, 'Father, I have sinned against heaven and before you; I am no longer worthy to be called your son.'* [22]*But the father said to his servants, 'Bring quickly the best robe, and put it on him; and put a ring on his hand, and shoes on his feet;* [23]*and bring the fatted calf and kill it, and let us eat and make merry;* [24]*for this my son was dead, and is alive again; he was lost, and is found.' And they began to make merry." (Lk 15:11-24 RSV)*

Patterns in the Prodigal

1. He lived with a "give me" attitude (v. 12).
2. He went into a far country (v. 13).
3. He squandered himself and his wealth (v. 13).
4. He lived out of step with what was best (vv. 14-16).
5. He came to his senses (v. 17).
6. He returned home (v. 18).
7. He confessed his sin (v. 18).
8. His father forgave him and put on a party (vv. 20-24).

Parallel Patterns in Us

1. We press for our independence.
2. We travel away from God.
3. We are harmful to ourselves and others.
4. We live in conflict with our Creator's plan.
5. We realize life is not right apart from God.
6. We can move back toward God.
7. We must confess and repent of our sin before God.
8. Our heavenly Father is anxious to forgive us through

Christ and plan a party to welcome us back to himself.

Making the big commitment. The following plan is developed around the analogy that becoming and being a Christian is like falling in love and getting married.

The Courtship Stage

1. Checking out Christianity's potential.
2. Beginning a friendship with Jesus.
3. Chasing away the doubts.
4. Falling in love with the Savior.

The Wedding Day

1. Making commitments and saying "I do."
2. Embracing your partner.
3. Signing the covenant with the Father.
4. Celebrating with the family of God.

Living in the Marriage

1. Growing in the relationship to Christ as Lord.
2. Living out the love of Jesus.
3. Saying "no" to other love affairs.
4. Adding to the family of believers.

True liberation. "I want to be free" is a cultural chant. Thus, an effective way to present the gospel is to call people to freedom in Christ. Dealing with the subject of freedom is not a simple matter, however. It is like unpacking a suitcase full of clothes that are knotted together.

Background Thoughts

1. Total freedom is a myth; freedom has built-in limits. For example, we can only express ourselves within the framework of the natural and moral laws that rule our existence. Just as we are unable to jump off the Empire State Building without falling, we cannot live selfishly without taking the consequences.

2. God is the only one who is totally free. He can express himself within his created, natural laws, or he can move

outside and perform miracles at will.

Discussion Starters

1. Is freedom simply the prerogative to do what we want without restraint?

2. Can we be free without the resources to implement our choices?

3. According to 2 Peter 2:19, we are slaves to whatever has mastered us. If we are mastered by whatever is most important to us, the central question is not

"How can we be free?"

but

"What are we going to serve?"

The Truth about Freedom

Christian teaching contends that we cannot be free if we try to function outside God's purposes.

1. Apart from God we are slaves to sin and other powers (Rom 6:16-18; Jn 8:34).

2. Jesus is our freedom fighter (Lk 4:18; Jn 8:35). We are freed from

☐ estrangement from God

☐ penalty for sin

☐ selfishness

☐ pride and egotism

☐ hate and unforgiveness

☐ destructive competitiveness

☐ crippling guilt

☐ demeaning lust

☐ tyranny of money

☐ aimlessness.

We are freed to

☐ know and enjoy God

☐ pursue truth

☐ love and care

☐ serve

☐ encourage and affirm

☐ understand others

☐ appreciate ourselves

☐ celebrate life

☐ give

☐ fulfill our purpose.

3. The power of the resurrection is our energy source to help us express our freedom (1 Cor 15:56; Eph 1:15-23).

4. Followers of Jesus have the power to obey and the freedom to disobey (Jn 8:31-32; 15:9-11). True freedom is a gift from God. Jesus Christ is the only liberator. All other ways lead to personal prisons.

As you think through how you prefer to articulate a biblical plan of salvation, begin to "chatter the gospel." Ask a Christian friend to listen and check you out. Let your friend play the role of a non-Christian. Then reverse the roles and try to think and respond as an unbeliever. Talk to yourself . . . rehearse in front of a mirror . . . do whatever you must to build your confidence and comfort when verbalizing the gospel. Pray that God will give you opportunities to share his good news in a natural way with the people who are part of your daily life. Your prayer will be answered!!

5. Count on the Christian Community

Our discipleship group was committed to practice the theory we talked about. We not only surrendered ourselves to the teachings of Christ and the authority of Scripture, but we had a sense of being accountable to each other. One evening as we were reporting and sharing our concerns, Susan requested prayer for her non-Christian sister who was seriously ill. Our questions to Susan unmasked a series of complex circumstances. Her marriage had alienated her sister from the rest of the family. The couple was facing crippling medical expenses, and the pressures were threatening their shaky relationship. Beyond praying, we asked how we could help. Someone suggested we show our care by giving Susan money to pass on to her sister to help with hospital bills. Our group combined their resources to collect several hundred dollars.

At the next group session, Susan was in orbit. She had gone home and spent the weekend with her sister. She played back how she had given her our gift on Friday evening. Her sister had been staggered that people who did not know her and who would probably never meet her, had given her money—especially since they were students!

The next morning, Susan's sister raised the matter of why her friends had been so generous. "People just don't do that kind of thing," was her charge. For the first time, Susan let her know that her friends were serious followers of Jesus. That revelation opened the door for a long discussion about God and what it meant to be a Christian.

Sunday morning, Susan made her final hospital visit before returning to school for Monday's classes. Her sister greeted her with a smile and an announcement. "Well, I guess our family now has two Christians. I prayed for a long time last night, and I want to follow Jesus too."

While the rest of us were blinking back our tears, one member of our group exclaimed, "That's the best twenty bucks I've ever invested!"

Someone's becoming a new believer as a result of the influence of just one other Christian is rare. We are privileged when we are the last link in the chain before someone connects with Christ, but we will seldom be the only link. The work of the Spirit is normally complemented by a network of God's people. God doesn't expect us to fly solo in our efforts to evangelize.

6. Develop Relationships and Organize Events

God honors the believers who enjoy relationships with friends who do not know Christ. We do not seek friendship just to create opportunities to influence people toward Christ. Our motives are not to be smudged with the dirt of calculating, "I will become your friend so I can talk to you about Jesus." God created us for relationships. Friendship is one of God's great gifts for us to enjoy. But restricting ourselves to Christian friends cuts us off from some of God's good gifts. And cutting ourselves off from significant relationships with non-Christians precludes our being used by

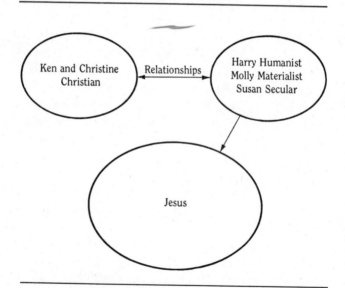

A few new believers flow directly out of significant relationships.

God to share himself with those who need him.

Organizational events are ineffective substitutes for significant relationships. Attempting to build the kingdom in the church or on campus with an events-centered ministry will fail. Posters and newspaper ads don't pull many people to events regardless of how well they are planned. Preoccupation with events will soon be counterproductive. Programs replace people. Resources are wasted. Incentive is destroyed. And those great crowds that mostly don't come, end up being ninety-nine per cent Christians who already believe that Jesus is "the way, the truth and the life."

Events can, however, provide an excellent opportunity

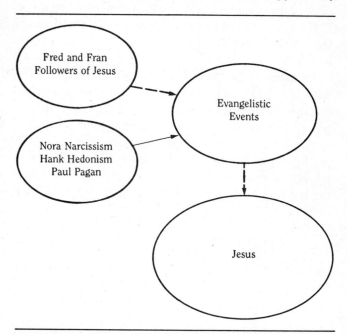

Events without relationships rarely result in new believers.

for unbelieving friends to take the final steps to faith. Most followers of Jesus are more effective seeders of God's truth than they are reapers of new believers. We shouldn't be surprised. The functions of planting and harvesting are radically different. This absence of personal reaping leaves a place for evangelistic events.

Events are best used to supplement the influence of our individual witness (see next page). When we bring our friends they are exposed to other Christians and our own witness is reinforced. Events are a means to an end and not an end in themselves. They serve the needs of a congregation or the members of a fellowship group rather than becoming the object of service. Most important, using events in this way commits us to a relational model for outreach. Our primary attention is to be given to people rather than programs.

In summary, we should involve the community of believers in the lives of those we hope will meet God. Introducing our friends to other Christians, discussing the contents of lectures, learning about Jesus in Bible discussions or Sunday school, going to church and sharing in worship, playing together and participating in weekend retreats—all register their impact for God. The corporate witness of the community of believers authenticates our individual witness.

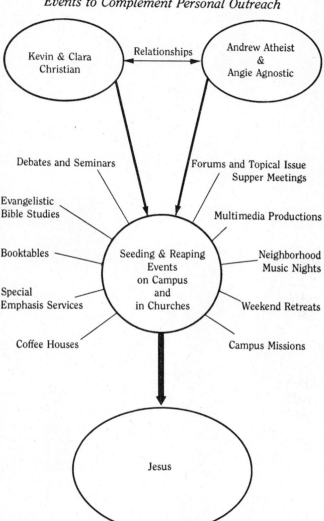

Events to Complement Personal Outreach

Kevin & Clara Christian

Relationships

Andrew Atheist & Angie Agnostic

Debates and Seminars

Forums and Topical Issue Supper Meetings

Evangelistic Bible Studies

Multimedia Productions

Booktables

Seeding & Reaping Events on Campus and in Churches

Neighborhood Music Nights

Special Emphasis Services

Weekend Retreats

Coffee Houses

Campus Missions

Jesus

Events which complement relationships will be fruitful.

5

LIVING LIKE JESUS

*H*ave you ever been asked to bring a non-Christian friend with you to a church or campus event? That request often trips alarms in our personal security systems. We react with: Who can I invite? How many non-Christian friends do I have? Does Mark know me well enough to trust me? How will I feel if Terry says no? Does Juanita even know I am a Christian? Then there are doubts about the event: What will happen if I bring Rick? Will he be pressured? Will the program have class? Will Mrs. Clinebell give one of her impromptu testimonies? Will Jennifer feel comfortable? Will I be embarrassed? Will she still be my friend when it's all over?

We can exchange our ambivalence for confidence. God wants his people to live and relate in the world. He will help us do so, and that knowledge will quiet some of our fears. We can be strong, knowing that God is committed to go with us into secular society. Realizing that Jesus has been in the world before us and knows our circumstances will be reassuring.

Following Jesus into the World

Jesus was the son of a small businessman. His childhood contact with his father's customers gave him skills to relate to all kinds of people. He grew up in touch with real life. When he was in his twenties he negotiated deals with suppliers of building materials and shook hands on agreements with his own customers. Jesus was a man of the world.

As Jesus moved from the carpentry shop into the business of building his heavenly Father's kingdom, he was comfortable in his secular milieu. His ministry did not revolve around the synagogue. Although he worshiped regularly and accepted Sabbath speaking invitations, his focus was outside the church calendar.

Jesus was an itinerant. He moved in a variety of circles. He was at ease with tax collectors and government officials. His friends included prostitutes. He was more concerned about human dignity than social status. He stepped across cultural barriers and conferred full-person status to women. He ate bread and figs in farmers' kitchens and fried fish over campfires with the unemployed. He reasoned with the religious elite in the morning and preached in the streets in the afternoon. Rather than calling people to hear him speak inside four walls, he opened the door to himself and stepped out toward them.

The religious establishment wanted Jesus to be conventional . . . a few degrees to the right on the orthodoxy scale. Their code called for Jesus to be serious. Late-night wedding parties and turning water into wine didn't fit with piety. Their king had to have status. Jesus lived like a vagrant. He disqualified himself as their Messiah and had to be discredited.

"You eat with tax collectors and spend too much time with sinners. You and your men break the Sunday blue laws —and on top of that you drink too much!"

Jesus knew defending himself would be a waste of energy and emotion. He simply set the record straight. "Those who are well have no need of a physician, but those who are sick. . . . For I came not to call the righteous, but sinners" (Mt 9:12-13 RSV). "For the Son of man came to seek and to save the lost" (Lk 19:10 RSV).

Go Where I Have Gone

When the time came for Jesus to step aside as an active player, his signals to his team of followers were clear: "Go where I have gone; Do what I have done."

During the last week Jesus spent with his disciples, he dealt with important matters. He related to them like a coach who knows he will be away for the big game. Knowing the end was near, Jesus was alone with his starting roster in the upper room. The day was Thursday. Tomorrow he would die. He only had time to deliver his last-minute instructions. We find Jesus assuming the role of a priest— representing God to his people and representing his people to God. Jesus was on his knees, praying for his disciples.

⁶I have revealed you to those whom you gave me out of the world. They were yours; you gave them to me and they have obeyed your word. ⁷Now they know that everything you have given me comes from you. ⁸For I gave them the words you gave me and they accepted them. They knew with certainty that I came from you, and they believed that you sent me. [9]I pray for them. I am not praying for the world, but for those you have given me, for they are yours. [10]All I have is yours, and all you have is mine. And glory has come to me through them. [11]I will remain in the world no longer, but they are still in the world, and I am coming to you. Holy Father, protect them by the power of your name—the name you gave me—so that they may be one as we are one. [12]While I was with them, I protected them and kept them safe by that name you gave me. None has been lost except the one doomed to destruction so that Scripture would be fulfilled.

[13]I am coming to you now, but I say these things while I am still in the world, so that they may have the full measure of my joy within them. [14]I have given them your word and the world has hated them, for they are not of the world any more than I am of the world. [15]My prayer is not that you take them out of the world but that you protect them from the evil one. [16]They are not of the world, even as I am not of it. [17]Sanctify them by the truth; your word is truth. [18]As you sent me into the world, I have sent them into the world. [19]For them I sanctify myself, that they too may be truly sanctified. (Jn 17:6-19 NIV)

This teaching tells us how followers of Jesus should see themselves in relation to the world.

1. Followers of Jesus come out of the world. Jesus begins his prayer by asserting that his work on earth has been completed. As he moves his attention to the disciples, Jesus thinks back to his first contact with them three years earlier when he called them "out of the world."

In our time, Jesus' invitation to believe in him calls people from the same place . . . out of enemy territory where
God is disregarded . . . out of Satan's turf where truth is
disbelieved . . . out of the secular environment where selfishness rules . . . out of darkness to light. The church of
Jesus Christ has always moved from alienation in the world
back into relationship with the Father. The Greek word
ecclesia which we translate "church" literally means "the
called-out ones." They are the ones who have turned from
the power of Satan to the power of God. Followers of Jesus
still come out of the world.

2. Followers of Jesus are sent back into the world. God's
surprise and Satan's great con job is wrapped up in Jesus'
single statement to his Father, "As you sent me into the
world, I have sent them into the world." God is unconven-
tional. After wooing us out of the world, he pulls the un-
expected and sends us back to the territory we just left.
Satan traps us with a more normal strategy. He wants to
keep God's redeemed people out of his territory to cut down
on his losses. His device is to sell the idea that the followers
of Jesus should huddle together in a closed community
away from the world.

We err when we conclude that the primary purpose of
the gospel is to get people out of the world and into heaven.
Just as Jesus left heaven to invade earth, within our space
and time God wants to move from heaven to earth by living in his people. His strategy is to keep his influence in our
broken world that so desperately needs to be rescued.

3. Followers of Jesus are to stay in the world. Listen to
Jesus' pleading tone: "My prayer is not that you take them
out of the world. . . . I will remain in the world no longer,
but they are still in the world." Jesus views his followers as
his replacements. We are to register a presence where he

left his mark. We are to do the same things Jesus did when he was in the world.

Jesus' teaching in this area is consistent. On other occasions he emphasized the same message:

☐ "You are the light of the world" (Mt 5:14 RSV). Live in the world, exposing darkness and revealing what is right and best.

☐ "You are the salt of the earth" (Mt 5:13 RSV). Live in the world as the spice of life.

☐ "You are yeast and leaven" (see Mt 13:33). Live in the world disrupting the status quo and sometimes disturbing the peace.

This same intent is present in 2 Corinthians 2:15 as God's people are asked to be the "aroma of Christ . . . among those who are perishing" (RSV). In this case, followers of Jesus are placed in the world as the perfume of love, service and truth.

4. Followers of Jesus are different from the world. Jesus' twist in his teaching about our relationship to the world comes with a double emphasis and caution on behalf of his disciples: "They are not of the world any more than I am of the world. . . . They are not of the world, even as I am not of it."

Some have interpreted Jesus' instruction to be "not of" the world as a directive to "get out" of the world. They have fostered a distrustful disposition that we must escape the world in order to survive as Christians in a non-Christian culture. But John 17, Jesus' teachings in other instances and his personal pattern denounce the escape mentality.

Jesus' directive to be "not of" the world is a call to be different from the world. The teaching gives Christ's people a mandate to be qualitatively distinctive. Certainly the distinctiveness will mean that followers of Jesus will abstain from the sinful practices of the world. We will be different because we "don't do" some things. Our more powerful impact, however, will result when we do some things that go beyond the norms of our bent-out-of-shape society. Not being worldly as Jesus was not worldly will be our aim. Overcoming evil with good will hit the target.

5. *Followers of Jesus are protected in the world.* If the double emphasis to be "not of" the world is a caution, then the repetition in Jesus' prayer for the protection of those in the world is a promise: "Holy Father, protect them by the power of your name. . . . Protect them from the evil one."

Satan wields power in his world. Living in the secular scene is dangerous. Risks of contamination are real. Temptations to be disloyal to Jesus are the world's specialty. The naive will be attacked in enemy territory. Some well-intentioned soldiers of the cross will be shot down. Yet in spite of the dangers and risks, Christ's mission is still in the world. And if Christ's mission is the church's mission, then the mission of the church is also in the world.

God's presence and commitment is enough to overcome the odds and to triumph in battle.

I am in you.

I will go with you.

I will never leave you or forsake you.

Let's go into the world together.

6

CONNECTING WITH CULTURE

A few weeks ago, part of my afternoon was spent in the plush offices of a manufacturing firm with the president and vice president of the company. Gene has served as the president for nearly twenty years. Jim has been the vice president during the entire time. Both men are committed believers in Christ.

Gene's home background was the "pure pagan" variety. His teen-age and university years were godless and lived without restraint. His manner is still on the loud and abrupt side. Gene refers to himself as an unlikely candidate to get involved with religion. However, a few years ago, while moving into his early forties, Gene surrendered himself to

Christ. His journey with Jesus has had some roller-coaster segments but today his witness is bold and effective.

Jim's story is the reversal of Gene's experience. He was born into a solid Christian family. As a young teen-ager he placed his faith in Christ. His movement toward God has been consistent. His vocational achievements earned him respect. His pleasant manner and social graces make him an enjoyable friend. Members of his evangelical church view him as a strong Christian leader. During the afternoon, our discussion included an account of the church boards and committees that receive Jim's regular counsel.

I knew Gene had a private word to deliver when he walked me to the parking lot. His message still lingers in my mind in a haunting and disturbing way. Gene's voice was subdued and almost remorseful as he spoke: "My becoming a Christian was traumatic for Jim. You know—we worked side by side for over ten years and he never said a word to me about Jesus. And I never met any of his Christian friends."

Rather than following Jesus into the world Jim, by his sin of silence, kept Jesus out of the world—the world he laid down his life to invade. Even though Jim worked in the world and had direct contact with the world, he separated his life in Christ from the place where he spent most of his time. He lived in two different worlds that never met because he played two different roles.

We need not elaborate on the sin of silence. We are not even tempted to feel superior to Jim. Rather, we bend our own knees to confess the same sin. We plead guilty to being silent when we should have revealed our identities as Jesus' people. In the same breath, we express our gratefulness for our forgiving God and his grace and refusal to give up on us. When I reflect on the many times my mind has signaled "speak" and my mouth has remained silent, I am embarrassed and ashamed. But thanks be to God for the sufficiency of the death of Christ that covers our sin and inconsistency.

The more complex problem that Jim showed in his relationship with Gene was his sin of isolating his faith from important departments of his life. Followers of Jesus are prone to live in circles of Christian containment.

Christians in Containment

Contained Christians live with a ghetto mentality. They feel out of place once they leave their Christian turf. They feel they don't belong. Away from their primary environment, they are always on the fringe of insecurity. Outside their circle, they are beyond their comfort zone.

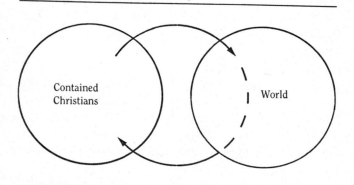

Christians contained by the church focus their lives around the church calendar and involvements with people from the church. Believers of the same breed on campus orient their lives around the programs of their denominational or parachurch organization. In both instances, these Christians count on the Christian community to meet all their needs. They share their lives "in Christ" at the cost of excluding others "outside Christ." They worship together and travel in caravans to retreats. They play with the people with whom they pray. They search for Christian plumbers and dentists. They eat lunch with each other in crowded cafeterias. They take vacations at the same times in the same places. They spend New Year's Eve at the watchnight service and New Year's Day watching football on television and eating in each other's homes. Christians in containment socialize and fraternize—always together. Eventually they form subcultural groups within the culture.

Contained Christians have some contact outside their circle of believers, but the essence of their existence is focused inside. They visit secular society to get what they need out of the world without really living there. Somehow life outside the circle doesn't count as much as life inside. Outside involvements are in the means-to-an-end category. For example, working in the world is necessary. Money is essential for carrots and cauliflower, to pay the rent and tuition and to give the tithe in order to support the more important work of the church. For the contained Christian, society is the place you go to pull someone back inside the circle or to make an occasional evangelistic raid. Otherwise, you try to keep your identity with Jesus as quiet as possible.

The mind of the contained Christian is set on the dial of survival rather than on penetration. He fears getting influenced and does not worry about being an influence. She prefers to sneak into the world and get out again without really being noticed.

Christians who live in containment regularly confuse the biblical teaching on separation with cultural isolation.

They conclude that separation from the sinful ways of the world is justification to get out of the world. Rather than going where Jesus has already gone to be an influence for God and good, their tactic is to escape. Abandonment of the world produces tragic results.

One result of containment is weakness. The longer Christians live in containment, the weaker they become. Christ gets squeezed out of large and crucial segments of their lives. The faith gets fragmented rather than integrated into the whole person. When Christ is forced out of sections of life other forces move in and take over.

The other tragedy of Christian containment is that Christ is kept out of our world. The reason for his death and resurrection is put on hold. Jesus is pushed to the sidelines of our culture. He stands in the churchyard looking over the fence at the community outside, and he grieves.

A "No News" Gospel

There is another matter worth grieving over that has come in the back door of our evolving society. This concern is the erosion of Christianity in our culture. In particular, the crisis centers on how the gospel is viewed by the majority of the population.

According to Canadian sociologist and statistician Reginald Bibby, twenty-five years ago sixty-seven per cent of Canadians attended church regularly. Today, church attendance has fallen to twenty-eight per cent. Looking at this twenty-eight per cent, we get even more concerned. According to the study, only twenty-two per cent of those who still have church contact would hold to the central elements of Christianity, such as belief in: God, the divinity of Jesus, life after death, the need for a personal experience with God, and the efficacy of prayer. An even smaller segment would characterize themselves as evangelical Christians.

In some ways the situation in the United States seems better. The majority of society believes in God. Millions consider themselves "born again." But what impact do these believers have on society? What sweeping changes are they making in favor of a more just government or foreign policy? It seems that while U.S. churches are growing, Christian influence on society is still shrinking. At the 1983 National Religious Broadcasters convention, theologian Carl F. H. Henry said, "In a culture where forty million to fifty million persons claim to be born again and where evangelists emphasize their growing harvest of conversions, the statistics of abortion, divorce, alcoholism and drug addiction, rape and murder nonetheless continue to mount. And a disconcertingly wide segment of American society succumbs to the premise that life has not come from God, doesn't move toward God and cannot be enriched by God."

Historically in North America Christianity has been the belief framework for the culture. Belief in the existence of God landed on the continent when the Mayflower docked. The idea that truth exists was an assumption of society well into the 1900s. As a result, until recent times, some things were right and others were categorically wrong. Jesus Christ was an important part of the total package. He was given a place and granted status. In the "good old days" the gospel was accepted by most as good news.

But just as a river in flood overflows its banks and cuts a new channel, industrialization flooded our culture and cut new channels of thought and experience. The scientific method preached a better way to verify what was factual. Ingenuity and productivity pushed up our standard of living and fed the notion that we had come of age. Our preoccupation with "what makes it work?" and "where can we use it?" sidelined the questions of "why?" and "why not?"

Computer designers and space explorers convinced us that we were all we needed. We took our "one small step for a man" and "one giant leap for mankind" from "in God we trust" to "in technology we trust." It was like traveling in a horse-drawn covered wagon on Monday and flashing a boarding pass for a 747 jetliner on Friday. We became more than our pride could resist. We were finally self-sufficient and in charge of our own destiny. The consequence for the gospel was the giant leap from being viewed as "good news" to becoming "no news" at all.

The "no news" claim needs to be qualified. In the past, the gospel was either "good news" or "bad news." God was either accepted or rejected. Neutrality was not an option. Today our situation has changed. The gospel is not examined and then accepted or rejected—it is ignored. Modern society has put any serious consideration of Jesus and the Bible in a museum with other relics from the past. The majority in society view the gospel as a non-issue.

But this is not our only problem. People outside Christian circles also have stopped listening to the voices proclaiming Christ in our culture. Repeated announcements about Jesus on bumper stickers, by television preachers and in Christmas carols have desensitized our society to the real significance of Jesus. Repetition has dulled the cutting edge of the truth about Christ. Right messages are being sent but not received. Lots of words are being declared but little meaning conveyed.

Consider what happens every Christmas in our society. Jesus gets more air time than the National Football League.

☐ On the radio, "Joy to the world, the Lord has come," moves up the charts into the top ten.

☐ In department stores, we shop to the lyrics of "O come to us, abide with us, our Lord Emmanuel."

☐ On television Christmas specials parade the regular cast of stars singing, "Peace on earth and mercy mild, God and sinners reconciled."

☐ Concert halls are sold out as Handel's *Messiah* is performed and musicians sing flawlessly, "Worthy is the lamb that was slain."

☐ We ride in elevators with music inviting us to "Come let us adore him, Christ, the Lord."

☐ At office parties, with carol sheets in one hand and glasses held high in the other, celebrations include, "Go tell it on the mountain that Jesus Christ is born."

Be assured—the truth about Jesus is being announced in our society. The gospel is being proclaimed. But the message is not connecting with our culture. In the eyes of the majority, Jesus has become another item on the list of cultural folklore. "Jesus Christ as Savior and Lord" has been lumped with "An apple a day keeps the doctor away" and "Cleanliness is next to godliness."

Gospel bullets packed with John 3:16 pronouncements do not connect with our culture. They are like missiles fired at random without guidance systems. They miss their targets and end up as unexploded and wasted ammunition. Shooting more bullets is not the answer.

Moving Back into the World

What is the answer to Christian containment, to the lack of Christian influence in society? Moving believers from their circles of containment into the world is part of the answer. As Christians live and move inside the structures of society, they will be able to influence people around them. Jesus will be connected with culture and regain a serious hearing as God's people faithfully represent him.

Escaping the world in a physical sense is difficult. Unless you choose the option of a monastic order or a convent, contact with the world is unavoidable. Taking a walk, shopping for groceries, going to school or finding a job necessitate venturing into society. Escaping the world in a psychological or social sense is a different matter. If you live in society with a hit-and-run mentality, you will keep the world at a safe distance. Relating to the world with your guard up will serve as a protective shield against relationships that count. Using the world as a supermarket to shop for the goods and services to make you comfortable back home will keep your focus out of the world.

But Jesus' teaching in John 17 will not allow us to tiptoe in and out of the world. We are to walk tall and straight with both feet planted firmly in our culture. We should reject the option of escape. We must listen to Jesus' firm voice: Go where I have gone. Get back into the world. Live in the world. Serve in the world. Work in the world. Make friends in the world. My mission is in the world.

Pagan society will never venture into our churches or seek out our campus groups. Instead, as the body of Christ disperses on Monday morning to go to work or school, the church ventures into our pagan culture. In God's game plan, wherever followers of Jesus *intersect* with the world, they will find their *place of mission* for Christ. Whenever followers of Jesus *interact* with people in the world, they will find their *opportunities for mission* in Christ.

The intersection between the church and the world is the action center for evangelism. The church is active when God's people are interacting with people in the world. Shared experiences at work and morning coffee with neighbors build rapport. As relationships develop with colleagues

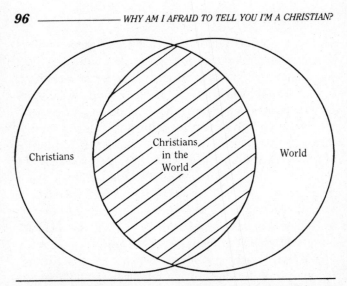

and classmates, there emerge appropriate opportunities to respond to people and care for individuals. As life is genuinely shared in the world, respect develops and trust builds. As we foster friendships over lunch and in the physical education building, discussions come naturally. We will find natural openings to tell the truth about life's issues and what Jesus has done. God honors these discussions and is present in these relationships. The Holy Spirit acts. The purpose of the cross will be fulfilled. The power of the resurrection is unleashed as people place their new faith in Christ.

If you have been living as a contained Christian, you need to change. Your past "ghetto" lifestyle may preclude a better future. You may have to consider changing jobs or moving to a different neighborhood to make a fresh start. Looking for new roommates might be an option. Moving from containment to contact in the world may come out of a new covenant with God "to let yourself be known." Here are some suggestions of how to get involved with people who don't know Jesus:

☐ Canvas in your neighborhood or school for the Cancer Society or Heart Fund.
☐ Offer your services as a Block Parent.
☐ Coach a community sports team.
☐ Help out in a political campaign.
☐ Join a service club.
☐ Go back to the same beauty salon or barber shop.
☐ Train to serve on a distress hotline.
☐ Become a member of a craft society.
☐ Join a campus special-interest club.
☐ Choose to live in a university residence.
☐ Try out for an all-school team.
☐ Participate in the intramural sports program.
☐ Join the staff of the campus newspaper.
☐ Play squash or racquetball at the local YMCA.
☐ Join a bowling or curling league.
☐ Take a night-school course.
☐ Run for local office.
☐ Volunteer to coordinate candy stripers for the hospital auxiliary.
☐ Deliver Meals on Wheels.
☐ Invite neighbors to a backyard barbecue.
☐ Host a carol sing for your block at Christmas.

In whatever measure you share your life with other people they will share their lives with you. As you openly take Christ with you into your relationships and the events of your days, you will share him as an extension of your real self, and his kingdom will come in you and around you.

Loving the World

What Jesus taught his followers about his kingdom, he

taught by example. His life was a statement of his theology. What he announced with his lips, he practiced with his hands and feet. Jesus was not a do-as-I-say leader. His style said: Come with me. I will show you.

As Jesus continues to bring his kingdom into being in our time, he works on the same principle. He commits himself to people who come out of the world. Then he declares:

Go where I have gone,

Do what I have done—and

I will be with you.

In Luke 9 Jesus called the twelve disciples together. "He gave them power and authority to drive out all demons and to cure diseases, and he sent them out to preach the kingdom of God and to heal the sick" (vv. 1-2 NIV). Jesus gave his disciples the authority and power to do what he was already doing. In this case, the Twelve followed his directives. "So they set out and went from village to village, preaching the gospel and healing people everywhere" (v. 6 NIV).

After being out on the road and spending time away from Jesus, the disciples were called back for a debriefing session (v. 10). The men had been looking forward to some private time with their leader. They made a rendezvous at a remote village. Intimacy with Jesus was their plan and hope. They had some great stories to tell.

Just as the telephone always seems to ring as you sit down for a quiet meal, crowds gathered when Jesus was in town. On this occasion five thousand men arrived with their families. Jesus took the interruption in stride. He taught and healed and spoke on his favorite subjects (v. 11). Late in the afternoon, the disciples ran out of patience.

"Jesus, enough is enough. Send the people away. It is

supper time. They need to go home or find a place to sleep."

Jesus managed to keep his patience under control. "I've got a better idea," he responded to his men. "You give them something to eat" (v. 13).

When the excitement was over and the disciples were finally alone with Jesus, the only story that seemed significant was the one about all the food that was left over after the surprise banquet.

Jesus repeatedly responded to people's needs. He not only laid down his life on the cross, he surrendered his daily agenda to the demands of hurting people around him. He was intent on demonstrating physical care for people. The gospel was more than words for Jesus. Touching blind eyes, healing sick bodies and feeding hungry stomachs were on his priority list.

In the situation described in Luke 9, Jesus' disciples wanted the crowd to leave so they could have their Master to themselves. But Jesus' attention was on the crowd around him. He sensed they were hungry. He knew the loving response toward hungry people was to feed them. So he laid a feast.

If we look to Jesus as our model for our verbal witness, we must also follow him as our example in life. The tangible expression of love was central to Jesus' understanding of life. Luke 10:25-37 underscores Jesus' commitment to the love ethic. On that occasion, Jesus was in a crowd when a lawyer cross-examined him: "What must I do to inherit eternal life?"

Jesus responded with his own question. "What is written in the Law? How do you read it?"

The lawyer replied, "Love the Lord your God with all your heart and with all your soul and with all your strength and with all your mind; and, Love your neighbor as yourself."

Jesus affirmed the lawyer's answer with his own shrewd reply. "Do this and you will live."

The lawyer pressed his case and asked for clarification about who qualifies as a "neighbor." Jesus seized the situation to tell the parable of the Good Samaritan.

"A man was going down from Jerusalem to Jericho, when he fell into the hands of robbers. They stripped him of his clothes, beat him and went away, leaving him half dead. A priest happened to be going down the same road, and when he saw the man, he passed by on the other side. So too, a Levite, when he came to the place and saw him, passed by on the other side. But a Samaritan, as he traveled, came where the man was; and when he saw him, he took pity on him. He went to him and bandaged his wounds, pouring on oil and wine. Then he put the man on his own donkey, took him to an inn and took care of him. The next day he took out two silver coins and gave them to the innkeeper. 'Look after him,' he said, 'and when I return, I will reimburse you for any extra expense you may have.'

"Which of these three do you think was a neighbor to the man who fell into the hands of robbers?"

The expert in the law replied, "The one who had mercy on him."

Jesus told him, "Go and do likewise."
(Lk 10:30-37 NIV)

The Good Samaritan is Jesus' love parable. His hero in the story gives us an artist's view of what love looks like:

☐ Love sees needs and stops.

☐ Love reschedules busy days.

☐ Love is compassionate.

☐ Love surrenders to the needs of hurting people.

☐ Love gets its hands dirty for others.

☐ Love costs . . . Love signs blank checks.

When followers of Jesus are lovers of the world, words are sometimes unnecessary. Love expressed in tangible terms is the final word. Love in action is truth demonstrated with resurrection power.

Last semester, Denise's classmate Gwen was crushed when her romance came to a sudden halt. The man in her life moved out. Her grades dropped dramatically, and she skidded into depression. Gwen was the strong, invincible type who had always been able to work out her own problems. But one day over lunch with Denise, Gwen literally cried in her sandwich and confessed her shattered state. Denise listened carefully. She didn't say much, except, "Why don't you move in with me? We can study together. At least you'll like my mother's cooking."

Denise and her family were serious Christians. Her gesture of friendship was accepted. Gwen moved in at the end of the next week. At first she was nervous, but that was quickly relieved. She sensed the family could absorb another person or two if the need was there.

Denise and Gwen studied together, shared some social life and allowed each other the freedom to keep contact with their own circles. Late one night, Gwen took the lead to talk with Denise about what kept her life together and what made her family the way they were. Two months later, Gwen announced at the supper table that she had joined God's family. The meal turned into a party.

This semester, Gwen is back on campus, living in a residence hall and attending a small-group Bible study on her floor. When she was asked what the major influence was in becoming a Christian, her answer was precise: "Denise's uncensored acceptance and her family's personal care."

The ultimate expression of the Christian life is to love.

There is no greater evidence of the life of Christ in any believer than being like the Good Samaritan. As followers of Jesus live out that kind of love, they act like Jesus himself.

Our society has raped love of its real meaning. In secular terms, the word *love* sends two messages:

1. Love is a feeling word . . . an expression of emotion. Love generates warm vibes between people. Hormones do handstands and genes jump with delight. People who are in love are romantically dazed. They feel good.

2. Love is a sex word . . . a reference to a physical act. *Making love* is a synonym for "having intercourse." Love is regularly used in song lyrics and in conversations among respectable people as a verbal symbol to denote sexual activity. Love is also confused with lust.

Biblically understood, love is distinct from an emotional sensation or physical experience. Love is defined in behavioral terms. Jesus is a model of what a life of love looks like. "Love is patient and kind. Love does not envy or boast. Love is not rude and self-seeking. Love forgives and rejoices in the truth" (1 Cor 13:4-7, paraphrase).

Love is commanded by a God who describes himself as love (1 Jn 4:8). God's command to love lifts the expression of love above the instinctive flow of an emotion. While emotional content is not drained out of Christian love, God's command is elevated to a matter of choice. Love is a willful decision to behave as God directs, using the energy his Spirit provides.

Living the life of love is Jesus' strategy for his followers. It makes them different from the world. In a society that is focused on self and preoccupied with vested interests, the Christian distinctive is to focus on others. Love behaves that way. In a greed-motivated society, the Christian is "not of" the world by giving instead of grabbing. Love acts that way. In a world that is careless about truth and justice, the Christian preserves what is true and fights for what is fair. Love connects truth with justice and appropriate action. In a world that lacks compassion, the Christian distinctive is sensitive care. Love reaches out with a personal touch. Love is God's weapon:

to overcome evil with good;

to beam light into the darkness and make the gospel "news" again.

But just as verbal witness needs to be adapted to the situation, love must correspond to circumstances. Hungry mouths are not loved when they are given warm coats. Neither are lonely people loved by our signing checks made out in their name.

Several years ago, I walked around the University of Alberta campus with a dissatisfied spirit. I felt that the Inter-Varsity group on campus had reduced the Christian life to words. I remember standing in front of the student union and praying out loud, "God, how can we demonstrate our theory? How can we love this campus for you?"

At that moment, two international students sauntered by. In the next sixty seconds God's Spirit connected my desire with an idea. "International students: What do they need? What do they face on arrival in our country?" The answer: *"Furniture*—that's what they need. They arrive with two large suitcases and a claim check for a trunk that comes later."

Several weeks later, our "Furniture Depot" was complete. Two IV group members coordinated the venture. The university students donated several thousand dollars to fund the cause. The student council gladly authorized a grant, and the university donated warehouse space. Used furniture was solicited from the community. The coordinators arranged for newspaper coverage and explained the international student predicament in television interviews. Students volunteered to drive trucks and pick up refrigerators, stoves and sofas in the evenings. During August and September, over a hundred international students and their families were welcomed with beds and tables and kitchen utensils in the name of Christ.

What began as a Furniture Depot is now a Winter Clothing Depot. The secret is out: students on the campus, along with university administrators, know that God's people care about other people who have needs. I will always remember receiving a letter from the president of the university. He was writing about another matter, but the first paragraph included the statement, "We have observed that the Inter-Varsity Christian Fellowship students have a special concern for our international friends. Can you help us again?"

Our love must be expressed in context and be tied to real needs. Providing fur coats for international students in Arizona is not love, but organizing a tutoring center on campus may be. As God's people, we have the responsibility of figuring out how to love. Like the Good Samaritan, we must keep our eyes open. If loneliness is the need, hospitality is the loving response. That may mean popping corn and pouring Cokes in a residence hall every Thursday night. If alternative social activities are needed to help some people escape the Friday-night drinking syndrome, God's people provide options. If handicapped students need assistance to get to a class across campus, God's people push wheelchairs. Mother Teresa is not the only person who has been directed by God to lay down her life for others.

As followers of Jesus we need built-in radar systems to sense the needs around us. When divorce strikes up the street, we should be among the first to knock at the door offering to babysit the kids or cook extra meals. The urge to serve should be stronger than the temptation to judge.

If housing is the crisis, God's people make extra room in their homes and expand their families. When a business colleague is fired, we phone or visit and offer our resources and ourselves. Our commitment to love pushes us beyond being comfortable.

We pass on our styles to our children. We teach them to look out for the new student in their classes and be the welcoming committee. God's people turn outward to others rather than turning inward on themselves.

What we practice on a personal level will be transferred to the body of believers and vice versa. What we do as churches will set a precedent for our personal lives. As communities of believers we will respond to the needs in the neighborhoods surrounding our church buildings. We will offer day-care services for single parents. We will visit the aged in nearby apartment buildings. We will encourage support and serve at the crisis center for battered wives. People living in poverty of one kind or another will get the word about where they can receive genuine help. Attitudes that we cultivate toward our immediate communities will penetrate the global views we hold and responses we make.

As we figure out how to love in practice, we will be prodded by Jesus' conversation with the lawyer who had the right definition of love (Lk 10:27). We will remember how Jesus pressed him: "Do this and you will live." According to Jesus' logic, if to love is to live, then refusal to love is to die. We can think back to occasions when both personally and corporately we chose not to love, and the consequence was a form of death. We want life according to Jesus' plan.

Jesus did not just talk the truth. He did it. We only represent Christ adequately when we speak the truth with our lips and our lives—our words and deeds. People in the world will listen when we transmit on both frequencies. When we are like Jesus, we re-incarnate his presence in our world and lift him up to draw all people to himself (Jn 12:32).

CONCLUSION: SUBSTITUTING FOR JESUS IS AN HONOR

Reflecting the likeness of Christ is a noble aspiration. The idea of coming off the bench and substituting for Jesus is an honor. But our honest reaction is that we are not really like him. Even in his human form, we see Jesus in a category beyond us. His motives are clean; his I.Q. raises the curve; he is without sin; his personal needs don't get in his way, and he is certainly more spiritual than those of us who believe in him. We cast our ballots of unworthiness with John the Baptist—we are not fit to untie Jesus' sandals (Jn 1:27).

But Jesus won't let us escape on those terms. Our incompleteness is an inadequate excuse for silence. Jesus explained that his returning to his Father would usher in the new age of the Spirit, and his Spirit would be in us (Jn 16:5-11). The Scriptures instruct us that we are "partakers of the divine nature," and we have great "treasure" housed in our humanness (2 Pet 1:4; 2 Cor 4:7 NIV). Then we hear tough language from Jesus. "If anyone is ashamed of me and my words in this adulterous and sinful generation, the Son of Man will be ashamed of him when he comes in his Father's glory with the holy angels" (Mk 8:38 NIV). "Whoever acknowledges me before men, I will also acknowledge him before my Father in heaven. But whoever disowns me before men, I will disown him before my Father in heaven" (Mt 10:32-33 NIV). Jesus the realist—he tells us the truth again.

We have to be truthful with ourselves. We confess that we have been ashamed to speak out on Jesus' behalf. Our intentions to love people even as we have sensed their needs have succumbed to our lethargy. We confess our periods of coldness and insensitivity. On the other hand, we know our desire to love and serve our Lord is stronger than our fears and indifference. We want our commitment to obedience to overrule our feelings of failure and inadequacy. We gladly reaffirm our privilege of "acknowledging him before men." In partnership with God and each other, we are ready to be "the voice" (Jn 1:23) and tell people what God has done for them in Christ. And we will aim at doing our telling Jesus' way. Our Lord's life is our calling. "I have given you an example, that you also should do as I have done" (Jn 13:15 RSV).

Taking our cues from Jesus, we aim to personalize his message in our daily relationships without compromising the truth. We seek to raise issues and speak the truth about all matters. We try to lead conversations toward the critical issue of salvation. We will not restrict our witness to words. We will speak the language of love with our behavior. We will merge our lives of love with our verbal articulation of what is right and true. Our evangelism will be a way of living and relating rather than a program or special event. Our witness will be normal to our lifestyle.

We will engage in classroom discussions about behavior modification or about Skinner's determinism as we attempt to offer a Christian point of view. Over coffee, we will not fear conversations about sexuality and the shapes of our bodies. We will use the situation to point out that the quality of our inner life is more crucial than our physical appearance. When talking to a Muslim friend and comparing what we believe about Jesus, we will eventually declare, "One of us has the wrong information." When our roommate is depressed with guilt after a night of moral compromise, we will take initiative to ask why, to discuss God's standards and to offer Jesus' forgiveness. Whether we are offering God's perspective on an issue, presenting Christ as Savior or expressing love that touches a specific need, we will adapt our response to the person in the situation and trust God with the results.

Appendix I

BIBLE STUDY:
RECONCILIATION

1. Begin your Bible study with a word association exercise. Ask for the group members' responses to at least five different words. Be sure the word *evangelism* precedes *reconciliation*. Your list of words might include:
   - ☐ halloween
   - ☐ television
   - ☐ communication
   - ☐ evangelism
   - ☐ reconciliation
2. Discuss the group members' responses to each word. What were their emotional reactions to *evangelism* and *reconciliation*? How did they feel?

   Explore the reasons why responses to *evangelism* and *reconciliation* were different.

   Define *reconciliation*.
3. Read 2 Corinthians 5:16-21.
4. Isolate the statements that include the idea of *reconciliation*:
   - ☐ How did God reconcile us to himself? (vv. 18-19, 21)
   - ☐ What are the two results of being reconciled to God through Christ? (vv. 17-18)

□ What is the basis of our appeal to others to be reconciled to God? (v. 20)

□ What is our assigned role in our ministry of reconciliation? (v. 20)

5. The passage teaches that those who are reconciled to God through Christ are "entrusted with the message of reconciliation" (vv. 18-19).

What components of this message are contained in the passage?

6. How can those who are reconciled in Christ prepare themselves to convey the message of reconciliation to those alienated from God? Choose one suggestion that will help you be better prepared.

7. The passage speaks about reconciliation with God. But we know from study of other passages of the Bible that God wants people to be reconciled to each other as well. Identify situations and relationships that need to be reconciled

□ in our world

□ in our country

□ on your street or in your apartment building

□ in your church

□ in your campus fellowship

□ in your family

□ among your friends

□ between you and another person

□ between God and individuals you know

8. The passage also teaches that those who are reconciled to God through Christ are "given the ministry of reconciliation" (v. 18).

Who do you know who needs to be reconciled to God? to others?

How are you going to express your ministry of reconciliation in the next seven days? What are you going to do?

9. Indicate your intentions to the group. Pray together. Phone each other within five days to find out what has happened.

Appendix II

SPEAKING TO BOTH BELIEVERS AND NONBELIEVERS

When leading a Bible study, chairing a meeting or speaking to a group that includes Christians and those who believe otherwise, language is important. It can make everyone feel included in your talk, or it can exclude those who are not yet Christians. Communicating to both audiences without boring one or alienating the other is a God-honoring objective.

Things Not to Do

1. Avoid the assumption that every person in the audience is a Christian believer.

2. Avoid assumptions about what people know. Assume that they need to be told everything from where a book is located in the Bible to details about New Testament history.

Examples to avoid:

"You know about what happened . . ."

"Familiar to all of us . . ."

"Well-known passage to us . . ."

3. Avoid inclusive statements that alienate. They create an "I-don't-belong-here" reaction!

"Let's not forget that as Christians . . . we have been entrusted with the gospel . . ."

"Important for us Christians . . ."
"You and I as Christians . . ."
"As Christians, we . . ."
In prayers: "Thank you that we can come together as believers in Christ."

4. Avoid the temptation to compromise the full force of the biblical message. Tell the whole truth without a judgmental attitude. Let the spirit of God have the final word.

Things to Do

1. Develop a respect for each person's right to choose what he or she believes. This gives people the same right God extends, and it recognizes that when it comes to the Truth we are all still learning. We all still see through a glass darkly.

2. Be aware of the words you use. Avoid Christian jargon such as "saved" and generalities such as "Jesus is the answer." Monitor terminology. If you use technical terms, define or illustrate them:

Evangelism	Reconciliation
Calvinism	Arminianism
Conversion	Born Again
Gospel	Sanctification

Use simple language that communicates clearly, and look for fresh ways to communicate ancient truths.

3. Use conditional statements, such as:
"If you are a follower of Jesus . . ."
"If you are considering a personal response to Jesus . . ."
"Those who are believers will know . . ."
"God wants all of his creatures to make choices about . . ."

"God talk" is a hindrance to effective communication. Christian clichés build walls instead of bridges. Clean communication helps create an atmosphere of acceptance and an environment where God's Spirit can work.

Further Reading on Evangelism from InterVarsity Press

Evangelism: Now and Then   Michael Green applies lessons learned from the apostles to evangelism today—its methods, motives, power and message. *150 pages, paper, 394-5*

How to Begin an Evangelistic Bible Study   Ada Lum tells how Christians can initiate and lead an evangelistic Bible study with their non-Christian friends. *33 pages, paper, 317-1*

How to Give Away Your Faith   Paul E. Little gives practical advice for realistic communication of the gospel. *131 pages, illustrated, paper, 553-0; study guide, 9-18 studies, paper, 440-2*

Out of the Saltshaker   Rebecca M. Pippert writes a basic guide to evangelism as a natural way of life, emphasizing the pattern set by Jesus. *192 pages, paper, 735-5; study guide, 12 studies, paper, 532-8*

Tell the Truth   Will Metzger gives a comprehensive analysis of what it means for people to offer the whole gospel to the whole person, with practical suggestions for communicating the message of salvation. *188 pages, paper, 464-X*